I0056435

Essential Skills and Competencies for Supply Chain Professionals and Future Leaders in Asia

A Framework for Planning and Managing Supply Chain Talents

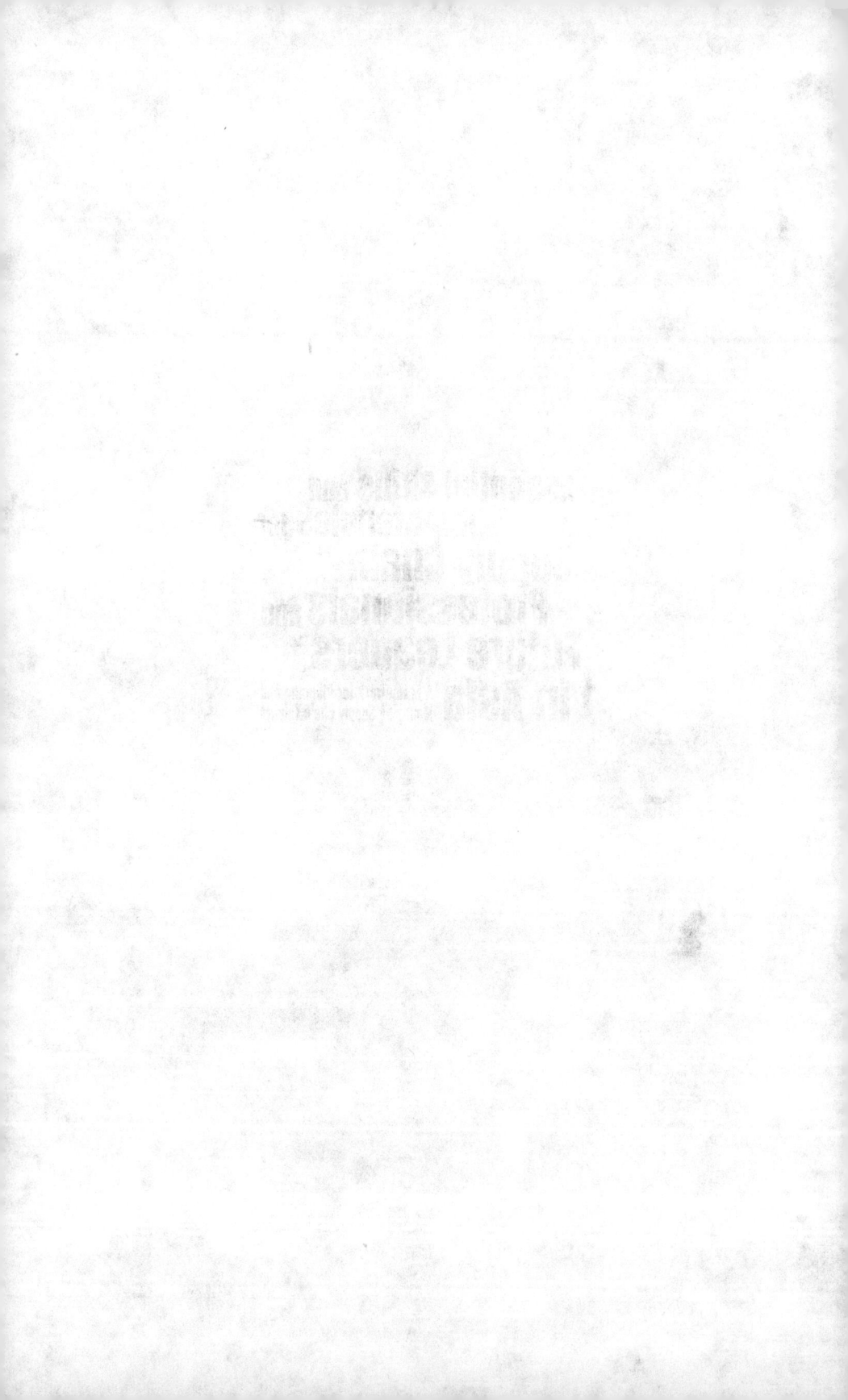

Essential Skills and Competencies for Supply Chain Professionals and Future Leaders in Asia

A Framework for Planning and Managing Supply Chain Talents

Editors

Albert Tan
Asian Institute of Management, Philippines

Sreejith Balasubramanian
Middlesex University, Dubai

Siti Norida Wahab
Universiti Teknologi MARA, Malaysia

World Scientific

NEW JERSEY • LONDON • SINGAPORE • BEIJING • SHANGHAI • HONG KONG • TAIPEI • CHENNAI • TOKYO

Published by

World Scientific Publishing Co. Pte. Ltd.
5 Toh Tuck Link, Singapore 596224
USA office: 27 Warren Street, Suite 401-402, Hackensack, NJ 07601
UK office: 57 Shelton Street, Covent Garden, London WC2H 9HE

Library of Congress Cataloging-in-Publication Data
Names: Tan, Albert Wee Kwan, 1962– editor. | Balasubramanian, Sreejith, editor. |
Wahab, Siti Norida, editor.
Title: Essential skills and competencies for supply chain professionals and future leaders
in Asia : a framework for planning and managing supply chain talents /
editors Albert Tan, Sreejith Balasubramanian, Siti Norida Wahab.
Description: Hackensack, NJ : World Scientific, [2023] |
Includes bibliographical references and index.
Identifiers: LCCN 2022022457 | ISBN 9789811258848 (hardcover) |
ISBN 9789811258855 (ebook for institutions) | ISBN 9789811258862 (ebook for individuals)
Subjects: LCSH: Business logistics--Asia. | Leadership--Asia.
Classification: LCC HD38.5 .E86 2023 | DDC 658.80095--dc23/eng/20220830
LC record available at https://lccn.loc.gov/2022022457

British Library Cataloguing-in-Publication Data
A catalogue record for this book is available from the British Library.

For any available supplementary material, please visit
https://www.worldscientific.com/worldscibooks/10.1142/12905#t=suppl

Desk Editor: Lai Ann

Typeset by Stallion Press
Email: enquiries@stallionpress.com

Foreword 1

There is an urgent need for business leaders to reimagine their supply chain function given the recent years of geopolitical and supply instability and disruptions, all of which have been further accelerated by the COVID 19-pandemic. And reimagining the capabilities to master the new-normal supply chains is what Dr. Tan and his co-editors have achieved with this book and the extensive research behind it.

The three editors present an insightful and modern view on what it takes to manage new-normal supply chains. The book provides a practical and relevant view on how business leaders and HR managers should think about recruiting, building, and retaining competent supply chain professionals. What this book also accomplishes is to provide a deep dive into what this means for companies, leaders, and supply chains in Asia. No past research or publications have gone into this depth on the supply chain capabilities required to operate in Asia. Their book clearly sets the standard on this topic.

What I found inspiring after reading this book is how the editors manage to translate the complexities of modern supply chains into practical guidance on what concrete skills are required to manage them. This should be seen in the context that supply chains have taken a major shift from "just being an engine room function" to being a mission-critical, customer-oriented business function that has earned its right at the executive table. It has become a function that, to a large degree, contributes to the performance, growth, and competitiveness of modern companies. Hence, it is important to understand exactly what capabilities are required with this function.

Therefore, I find it refreshing that this book looks beyond "the usual functional capabilities" such as inventory management and forecasting. It introduces the much-needed soft and managerial sides of being a successful supply chain professional, e.g., communication, change management and cross-cultural management, and blends it with the new-normal such as AI, machine learning, automation, analytics, and blockchain technologies. All of these are must-haves for a modern supply chain professional to successfully navigate through the disruptive environment that companies find themselves now and in the future.

In summary, the editors' insights and recommendations will guide and inspire business leaders, supply chain professionals and HR managers. It will serve as a welcome guide to navigate the jungle of what capabilities are required in the new-normal landscape.

Dr. Mads D. Lauritzen
EY-Parthenon Asia-Pacific Strategy and Transformation Leader

Foreword 2

With the rapid development of new information system and technologies, information can flow across the entire supply chain while data-driven decisions are enabled by artificial intelligence. Faced with supply chain disruptions due to the pandemic, many supply chain professionals are wondering what are the new key skills and competencies *for the future*. This book is timely to guide professionals on what skills are needed and how they can stay relevant in times of rapidly changing supply chain management.

Organizations operating globally have to get their supply chain professionals proficient in managing supply chain functions such as transportation, warehousing, inventory management, and production planning. This book extends traditional supply chain end-to-end functions within the firm to outside the firm throughout the value chain. It is well constructed, and readers can envisage revisiting specific chapters in isolation whilst constructing and delivering supply chain skills.

This book fills an important void in the current literature to identify the supply chain skills required by supply chain managers and leaders in Asia. In order to avoid habitual thinking traps and to meet future needs, a more comprehensive approach with quantitative and quality research in reskilling supply chain professionals to build new competencies for the new norm is required.

This book provides a framework for delivering guidance on the mental shift of the role of the supply chain executive from functional to process-focused, and for supply chain leadership to become part of the executive team. Supply chain managers and leaders can enhance or upgrade their skills based on the findings of this book, while HR managers can include these competencies when recruiting new supply chain professionals.

Ming Dong
Professor
Department of Management Science
Antai College of Economics & Management
Shanghai Jiao Tong University

Contents

About the Editors and Contributors

Albert Tan, PhD, CPIM-F
Asian Institute of Management
123 Paseo de Roxas, Legazpi Village, Makati, 1229 Metro Manila, Philippines
Email: atan@aim.edu

Dr. Albert Tan Tan is currently an associate professor at the Asian Institute of Management in the Philippines. Prior to that, he was an associate director managing the master's program in supply chain management and logistics management. His research works have been published in more than 60 international journals and was a senior editor for *Cogent Business and Management*. He has supervised the research of over 100 MSc students in supply chain management. Albert previously worked as a director in a government agency responsible for upgrading the IT capability of the manufacturing and logistics industries. He has also provided numerous ERP and reengineering consulting services for both discrete and process environments in Asia to streamline their supply chain while working for an IT vendor. He is a certified fellow in CPIM from APICS.

Janya Chanchaichujit, PhD
Prince of Songkla University (PSU)
Faculty of Environmental Management
Hatyai, Songkhla 90110, Thailand
E-mail: janya.chanchaichujit@gmail.com

Dr. Janya Chanchaichujit is an Associate Professor in Logistics and Supply Chain Management in the Faculty of Environmental Management, Prince of Songkla University in Thailand. Dr. Chanchaichujit holds a PhD in Logistics and Supply Chain Management from Curtin University in Australia, an MSc in Operational Research from the University of Hertfordshire in the UK, and BSc in Mathematics from Mahidol University in Thailand. Dr. Chanchaichujit has over 20 years of experience in logistics and supply chain management research and consultancy projects with a strong track record in securing funding from national and international funding agencies and the private sectors. She has successfully undertaken several projects in Thailand and the GMS region, including Green Freight and Logistics, Supply Chain Digitalization and Technology Adoption, and Agricultural Supply Chain.

Sreejith Balasubramanian, PhD
Middlesex University, Dubai
Dubai Knowledge Park — Blocks 4, 16, 17, & 19
P.O. Box 500697
Dubai, United Arab Emirates
Email: s.balasubramanian@mdx.ac.ae

Dr. Sreejith Balasubramanian is the founder and head of the Centre for Supply Chain Excellence at Middlesex University, Dubai. He is also the Chair of the Research Committee. He completed his PhD from Middlesex University Business School, London. His areas of expertise include supply chain, operations management, disruptive technologies, sustainability, and knowledge management. His work has been published in leading academic and practitioner-focused journals, including *Supply Chain Management: An International Journal; Production,*

Planning & Control; and *Journal of Knowledge Management*. He has been a consultant for several public and private sector entities and intergovernmental organizations including the Abu Dhabi Chamber of Commerce and Mekong Institute.

Siti Norida Wahab, PhD
Department of Technology and Supply Chain Management Studies
Faculty of Business and Management
Universiti Teknologi MARA
42300 Bandar Puncak Alam, Selangor, Malaysia
Email: sitinorida23@uitm.edu.my

Dr. Siti Norida Wahab is a senior lecturer in the operations management program at the Faculty of Business and Management, UiTM Puncak Alam. She has more than 15 years of experience in both the industrial and educational fields. Her previous leadership positions include roles at the managerial level in multinational logistics companies and renowned private universities. Her research interest includes sustainable adoption in logistics and supply chain management. She managed national and international grants and has published her research works in high-rated journals, proceedings, and book chapters. Besides, she supervised a number of MSc and PhD candidates. For excellence, she has won platinum, gold, and bronze medallist for the innovation competitions. She also actively serves as a reviewer for journals and academic conferences. Currently, she is a professional technologist of the Malaysia Board of Technologists and a chartered member of the Chartered Institute of Logistics and Transport.

Juliater Simarmata, PhD
Trisakti Institute of Transportation & Logistics
Jl. IPN Kebon Nanas No.2, RT.9/RW.6, Cipinang Besar Sel.
Kecamatan Jatinegara, Kota Jakarta Timur, Daerah Khusus Ibukota
Jakarta 13410, Indonesia
Email: juliaters@gmail.com

Dr. Juliater Simarmata is currently the Vice Rector of Trisakti Institute of Transportation & Logistics, Jakarta, Indonesia. His research works have been published in international journals. He is teaching entrepreneurship, business management, and marketing management. Dr. Juliater is a founder of tiket10.com (an e-commerce business system with 4,000 members in Indonesia), and the founder of Golden J Jewellery (design, production, and distribution).

Ms Hanh Thi Hong Nguyen,
Faculty of Business Administration, Ton Duc Thang University
19 Nguyen Huu Tho St, Tan Phong Ward, Dist. 7, Ho Chi Minh City 70000, Vietnam
Email: nguyenthihonghanh@tdtu.edu.vn

Hanh Thi Hong Nguyen (Ms) is a lecturer in international business at the Faculty of Business Administration, Ton Duc Thang University, Vietnam. She received her master's degree in Commerce with two specializations: Finance and Logistics — Supply Chain Management from the University of Sydney, Australia. Her research interests are digital transformation, international business strategy, supply chain management, and sustainability.

Sherman Ong, PhD
Master of Business Studies (Manufacturing & Logistics, 1st Class Honours, Overall Top Student), University College of Dublin, National University of Ireland; Doctor of Business Administration, University of Western Australia, Perth, Western Australia;
6, Clover Close, Singapore 579248
Email: drshermanong@gmail.com

Dr. Sherman Ong is an associate with several organizations. Principally, he engages clients in Gallup Strengths coaching, Project Management, Risk Management, Change Management, Supply Chain Management, and integration consulting and facilitating training to prepare clients for project management certification. Dr. Ong continues to speak at regional symposiums, seminars, and workshops, engaging C-level senior executives in enterprise-wide cultural transformation.

Sumit Mitra, PhD
Professor, Strategic Management
Indian Institute of Management Kozhikode
Kerala-673570, India
Phone (work): 0495-2809108
Email: smitra@iimk.ac.in

Sumit Mitra is a professor of strategic management at the Indian Institute of Management Kozhikode, India. He actively engages in researching strategic and competitive issues in value chain activities, corporate governance, and social entrepreneurship. His publications have appeared in refereed journals like *Journal of World Business*, *China and World Economy*, *Benchmarking: An International Journal*. Sumit has published book chapters and teaching cases. He holds a PhD in management from the Indian Institute of Management Ahmedabad, India. He has taught in India and abroad with administrative experience as a doctoral program chair and an academic board member. His corporate training and consulting experience include designing and executing training for public and private sector enterprises both in India and abroad.

Chapter 1

The Need for Supply Chain Professionals

Introduction

The aim of this book is to identify the supply chain skills required by supply chain managers and leaders in Asia and suggest the key skills and competencies that all supply chain professionals need to acquire. Supply chain executives used to be experts at managing supply chain functions such as transportation, warehousing, inventory management, and production planning. But the supply chain process extends end-to-end within the firm and even outside the firm **throughout the value chains**, including the relationships with suppliers and customers on a global basis. Leading firms now see the supply chain functional leader as the necessary executive to coordinate the end-to-end supply chain process, even though he or she does not control it all. The battle for top supply chain talent must be focused on acquiring people with process expertise, not simply functional competence. The mental shift to supply chain as a process leads inevitably to the shift of the role of the supply chain executive from a functional focus to process focused and to supply chain leadership becoming part of the executive team.

Supply chain managers and leaders can enhance or upgrade their skills based on the findings from this research while HR managers can include these competencies when recruiting new staff for supply chain professionals. We had conducted both quantitative and quality research for this study. For quantitative research, we conducted online surveys (see questionnaire in the Appendix A and B) for eight countries targeting 300–400 supply chain managers with more than 5 years of experience. Meanwhile, for qualitative research, we conducted one-to-one interviews with supply chain managers to confirm the essential skills and competency to be successful. We also extracted the skills requirements as listed from job advertisements posted on LinkedIn. This triangular method helped us to converge the essential skills and competencies, which are required to be a successful supply chain manager.

This is the first time that had attempted to identify the skills and competencies from Asia countries as most of the studies are conducted in the United States and Europe. McKinsey consultancy report in 2020 believes that leaders should take this moment not just to fix their supply chains temporarily, but to transform them. Reimagining supply chains to avoid past traps and meet future needs will require a more comprehensive approach in reskilling the supply chain professionals to build new competency for the new norm.

This book can also guide HR managers in setting criteria to hire new supply chain professionals based on the findings. We used the results from our survey, interviews with supply chain experts in Asia and from the job advertisements to arrive at the essential skills, and competencies that all supply chain managers need to equip to be successful.

This research aims to examine the questions of what skills and competencies are necessary for supply chain managers to be successful in their job and how these skills may change in the future. Triangulation is utilized in this study. The type of triangulation technique employed in this book is methodological triangulation, in which the authors used and combined qualitative and quantitative methods to obtain a comprehensive understanding and a wide and deep picture of the research question. The methods of data collection and interpretation used in this study are in-depth interviews in each of the country after the online survey is conducted. The survey questionnaire is divided into three skill categories, namely supply chain competency group, managerial competency group, and IT competency group as shown in Figure 1. Lastly, we extracted the skills requirements from the job advertisements for supply chain managers from Linkedin.com.

The survey questionnaire is pre-tested with some of the interviewees and all feedback is incorporated into a revised questionnaire. The finalized version is published online for all the potential respondents

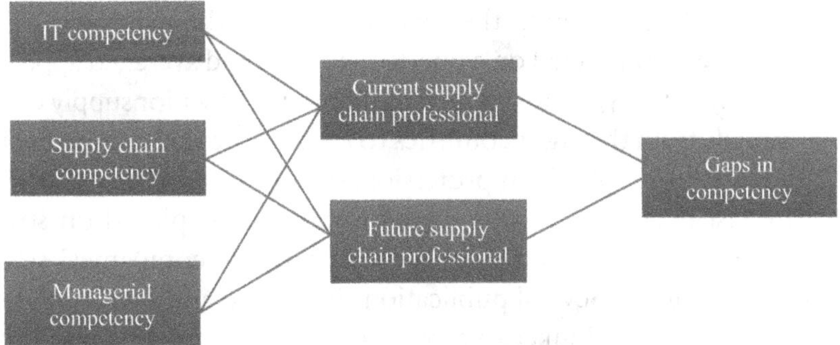

Figure 1: Identifying gaps in competency

from eight countries to reply. We expected 200–300 respondents for this online survey. The interviews with senior logistics or supply chain executives are selected on convenience basis, that is, from the authors' contact database or from members of related associations. Given the target population being supply chain professionals with their skills and knowledge as the unit of analysis in this research, the sampling frame for the questionnaire survey is constructed from the member directory of association with the total sampling approach taken or from the author's contact database.

Interviewees are asked to identify potential changes that may impact the skills and competency required by supply chain professionals in the future especially during COVID-19 pandemic. Some of the interview questions are listed below:

- What are the key goals and targets that you have set for your supply chain staff?
- What are the essential skills or competencies for decision-making for supply chain issues?
- Where do you see yourself in the next 5 years?
- Is there anything that you would like to add to be a competent supply chain manager?

Prior to the interviews, a list of prospective interviewees in various organizations was drawn up, and each of these interviewees was contacted via email inviting their participation in the interviews. The interviews were conducted on a one-to-one basis and averaged approximately 60 minutes. We had planned to interview 30 senior supply chain professionals from the eight countries to identify the skill competencies to be successful supply chain professionals.

The last data collection is through job adverts placed on social media sites such as LinkedIn, as well as from the companies' social media and websites. Several publications have used and discussed how to harvest data from LinkedIn as well as other social media platforms (Ben *et al.*, 2013; Case *et al.*, 2013; Prieto *et al.*, 2013; Dai *et al.*, 2015; Alruwaili and Alahmadi 2021). In their studies, they gathered information from LinkedIn accounts of people they knew. When categorizing the data that they collected, several academics used clustering to analyze the data (Dai *et al.*, 2015; Alruwaili and Alahmadi 2021). These publications have demonstrated that gathering data from social media can be a decisive method of research. The information that is acquired for this study will be information regarding job adverts for supply chain and logistics managers.

As previously stated, LinkedIn will be the main platform where the majority of companies post their job advertisements and will be the primary source of data; nevertheless, some job **advertisements** will be delivered by companies to people through other social media platforms. The information for this study was gathered through LinkedIn by searching the jobs section using the keywords "supply chain" "supply chain manager," "logistics manager," and "supply chain specialist," as the focus of this study. Supply chain managers is the topic of interest for the editors, and the keywords used are based on that subject. However, the editors are open to a variety of options so long as the keywords are related to or have a similar meaning to supply chain managers. Unfortunately, the search results for the keyword "logistics manager" are dominated by companies seeking logistics supervisors and warehouse managers. The editors selected viable samples from the search result, one of the criteria to determine a viable result would be job advertisements posted by well-known companies either locally or internationally.

Significance of the Book

Essential Skills and Competencies for Supply Chain Professionals

Although competencies have been extensively researched at the person and team levels, as well as more recently at the firm level, they have only been investigated infrequently (if at all) at the inter-organizational level, according to the authors. In general, competencies are assumed to be made up of knowledge, skills, and abilities that are connected with high levels of performance on the job at the individual level, according to conventional wisdom. This is especially true in the context of human resource management (Mirabile, 1997). Teams' competency is influenced by individual proficiency as well as one's capacity to interact with and learn from other members of the group. In accordance with a recent study, team talents include not only technical **competency** but also social competency, which is particularly important in teamwork and communication. When applied to four self-management team competencies, Kauffeld (2006) looked at knowledge, skills, ability to communicate and cooperate, and willingness to create a collaborative learning environment, as well as readiness to collaborate with others. As defined in this context, competency is defined as an internal activity that an organization is capable of carrying out expertly, and many skills (such as continuous product creation) are believed to be fundamentally multidisciplinary and cross-functional in nature (Koufteros *et al.*, 2010). As businesses attempt to meet the ever-changing demands of the business world, the perception of what constitutes talent will continue to develop and expand (Athey and Orth, 1999). Employees' competencies (knowledge, skills, and abilities) must be put into action in the form of behavior, resulting in outputs that produce outcomes. According to Parry (1996), employees must possess the following skills and abilities: Competencies–Behavior–Outputs–Results.

Finding capable human resources is a necessary but not sufficient criterion for successful HRM practices. More specifically, firms must facilitate congruence between a person's competencies and a job's demands, which is conceptualized as "person–job fit". Person–job fit has been positively associated with job performance and job satisfaction (Caldwell and O'Reilly, 1990). Accordingly, the employee selection practices of most organizations focus on achieving person–job fit. A central element of facilitating this match is the identification of job demands to enable recruiters to find the job prospect with the best match. Consequently, a fair share of HRM studies in SCM and logistics has focused on identifying and classifying the most important competencies and recognized it as key factor in human resource selection. Both literature streams of research on SCM and logistics competencies have been part of our comprehensive literature review for two reasons. First, although both professions need to be distinguished, there is considerable agreement among researchers and practitioners that they are closely related and demand similar competencies. Therefore, in order to achieve a great result in organizational performance, a company must employ a good supply chain manager to handle all the supply chain **processes** in the company.

Competencies Required for Supply Chain Managers

The provision of logistics and supply chain services is essential in every country, there are several logistics and supply chain companies that make major contributions to the economy of their home countries. There are also five phases being outlined in the new supply chain plans for achieving supply chain excellence and actual value, and they are as follows: hiring the right people, implementing advanced technology, collaborating with external partners, collaborating internally, and embracing supply chain innovation. Currently, market competition is more closely associated with a company's supply chain than it is with competition between individual enterprises. Because of this, successful SCM has evolved as a potent tool for achieving a competitive advantage in market competitions in recent years (Li *et al.* 2006). As a result, improving supply chain performance has emerged as a critical strategic priority for every organization competing in the market (Agami *et al.*, 2012). Green *et al.* (2019) discovered that the level of SCM adoption has a positive and statistically significant link with competitive advantage. As a result, many firms are turning to supply chain management (SCM) as a competitive weapon to boost performance (Sutduean *et al.*, 2019). The operational effectiveness of the supply chain will have a positive impact on both the environmental and financial performance of the organization (Simatupang and Sridharan, 2002). So, in order for logistics and supply chain companies to be successful, their employees must be highly qualified and professional in their roles. While traditional logistics functions such as logistics information systems, transportation, and warehousing used to be the primary focus of logistics professionals, today's logistics professionals must constantly interact with other functional areas within an organization, such as marketing and production, as well as those of their suppliers and customers, in order to ensure that the organization's value chain is maintained and optimized.

What becomes evident is that in order to be a great logistics manager, one may require superhuman abilities in order to handle a wide range of responsibilities. While a recent study by Carter *et al.* (2007) asserted that supply management organizations would play a more valuable role in the coming decade and that their success would depend on whether or not they were able to attract, develop, and retain individuals who possessed the skills and capabilities necessary to excel in the future. SCM can be used strategically to add value to a company if it is carried out properly (McCarter and Northcraft, 2007). When it comes to almost all company situations, SCM and human resource management are "intimately connected together" (Boudreau, 2002, p. 179). The competencies required of the supply chain manager, as well as the competencies required of the network itself, have received little attention to date (Gammelgaard and Larson, 2001). Since their first presentation by McClelland (1973) and Lawler (1994), the notion of competencies has grown in scope, extending from the field of human resource management to encompass a wide range of business disciplines.

The shortage of skilled supply chain managers will be a key challenge in the coming decade, according to Closs (2000), who forecasts that "a dramatic shift in logistics and supply chain education" will be required. Along with this, numerous studies were published during the 1990s that called attention to the wide range of abilities that logistics managers are expected to possess (e.g., La Londe, 1990; Williams and Currey, 1990; Murphy and Poist, 1991a, 1991b; Gibson *et al.*, 1998; Minahan, 1998; Trunick, 1998). And for the most part, logisticians today do not coordinate transportation, packing, storage, and inventory management as much as they did in the 1960s. Instead, a number of factors, such as globalization, computerization, and cross-firm relationship management, are driving the evolution of the logistician's role. And, unlike in the 1960s, there appears to be some agreement on the necessary abilities to deal with altering employment, with leadership being named as one of the most crucial to develop in today's workforce (Caplice, 2005; Hoffman, 2005; Skrip, 2006). It is becoming increasingly difficult for logistics managers to manage the supply chain as a result of the increased volatility and competition in the market environment. Handle the inherent paradox of cutting costs while simultaneously strengthening customer service while simultaneously improving customer and supplier relationships inside the supply chain, which further complicates matters (Christopher, 1999). What knowledge and skills logistics professionals require to deal with the broader challenges that come with their position in a worldwide economy is one of the issues that must be addressed. Moreover, logistics professionals must be multiskilled in a variety of management skills in addition to possessing a depth of logistical knowledge and abilities, which means they must possess both generalist and specialized knowledge and skills in the field of logistics (Gammelgaard and Larson, 2001; Razzaque and Sirat, 2001; Murphy and Poist, 2006).

Additionally, recruitment, retention, and succession planning are among the most difficult difficulties in SCM, mostly due to a lack of understanding of supply chain people and their requirements among enterprises and human resource management specialists (John, 2015). Improvements in understanding of critical SCM competencies would be mutually beneficial for both employers and employees, as it would enhance the possibility of matching job-related competencies and needs, which would benefit both parties. And with the globalization of business, many parts of the business have changed, and the industry has changed as well, particularly the demand for human resources in corporations. The supply chain and logistics industry are one of several that have been impacted; as a result, the skill sets and qualifications for supply chain and logistics managers have evolved as well. Because of the increased expectations, the Fourth Industrial Revolution (Industry 4.0) requires supply chain and logistics managers to engage in the use of technologies.

Industry 4.0 unquestionably transforms the way things have been done in the past into a new way of doing things, particularly in the supply chain. In **Industry 4.0**, the emphasis is on digitization and the Internet of things (IoT); people are more connected through the Internet; they frequently order products online and expect the items to be delivered to them; and they are more environmentally conscious. As a result, **Industry 4.0** presents a challenge to the supply chain, which must combine technologies and the internet in order to deliver products to clients or obtain them from suppliers in the first place. In addition to identifying methods of delivering items, supply chain managers are required to address the digital value chain and provide the products' value to the end users. Because the world is becoming more connected with one another, supply chain managers in Industry 4.0 must also be capable of obtaining information and communicating online. Industry 4.0 will revolutionize the business processes of all firms, including SCM. As a result, supply chain managers must consider how to create a new framework and design a new business process, or even how to completely restructure the companies involved with the supply chain. To be compliant with Industry 4.0, the supply chain must be reorganized. This includes changes in design, planning, production, distribution, consumption, and even reverse logistics, all of which are facilitated by the integration of technology and the Internet. Additionally, the term "Smart Logistics" is used in relation to SCM. Supply chain managers must be equipped with the necessary tools, means, and intelligent methods, as well as the necessary level of intelligence to apply and use these methods in order to keep the supply chain relevant in Industry 4.0.

These days consumers are getting more demanding, which makes the supply chain more difficult, according to a McKinsey & Company analysis. However, with the aid of technology, it will be able to meet customers' demands while also evolving the supply chain as a whole. Making the next supply chain generation more adaptable, strong, and long-lasting is the ultimate goal here. Agile and robustness are brought about by the use of technology, whereas sustainability is brought about by people's realization that they can meet their current needs without jeopardizing their future. While operations are currently the most important component of most firms, the supply chain will become the most important part of enterprises as businesses become more globalized and more connected to one another, bringing the world closer together. Ernst & Young (EY) (2021) has reported how the pandemic has caused disruption in the supply chain, resulting in the need for supply chain and logistics managers to reexamine their skill sets and qualifications. Supply chain and logistics managers must be able to ensure supplier reliability and secure their products at all stages of the supply chain in order to be successful. With more countries shutting down their factories due to COVID-19 virus, the supply chain is disrupted and supply chain managers need to find alternatives in sourcing their raw materials and services.

In a separate research, researchers find that logistics and supply chain managers must possess a wide range of abilities in order to be successful. People skills, analytic skills, communication skills, and computer skills (see Gibson *et al.*, 1998) have all been assessed, as have the 83 elements defined by Murphy and Poist (1991b) as business skills, logistical skills, and management skills (see Murphy and Poist, 1991b). Moreover, according to a number of additional studies (Young, 1998; LeMay, 1999), other abilities required for these managers range from technology to organizational and interpersonal skills. Managers' ability to combine and use their particular expertise for better organizational advantage has also grown increasingly significant as a result of the rise in the importance of organizational skills (Athey and Orth, 1999). These bundles of knowledge, skills, and abilities that are critical to the development and realization of organizational goals would appear to be particularly relevant in the field of SCM.

Murphy and Poist (1991b) identified the following skill sets and qualifications needed for senior-level managers in companies:

- Business skills. It is necessary for logistics executives to have expertise that is both directly and indirectly related to the company. Understanding of the functional areas that make up a business, as well as knowledge of subjects as diverse as economics, psychology, and sociology, are examples of what is required.
- Logistics skills. Managers will need to be familiar with a wide range of logistics industries, both large and small.
- Management skills. Managing logistics requires a combination of talents in planning and organizing, as well as personal characteristics that will allow them to be effective in this setting.

Due to the fact that SCM is concerned with coordinating the activities of all supply chain members in an effective and efficient manner, it is critical to create metrics that can be used to measure the results of management efforts for both supply chain members and customers. Performance is defined as the outputs and results of SCM research in the traditional sense (Chen and Paulraj, 2004; Closs and Mollenkopf, 2004). When compared to productivity and effectiveness, efficiency is an inward-looking indicator that displays how effectively resources are employed in the accomplishment of output goals (Lai *et al.*, 2002). A company's competitiveness is linked to the growth of its human capital, which includes the development of its employees' abilities as well as the development of core competencies that are unique, distinctive, and difficult to replicate (Barnes and Liao 2012).

It is clear from the literature that supply chain managers must possess a range of multidimensional skills and competencies to manage their complex, global supply chains and be in a position to deal with a wide variety of issues and challenges effectively and responsively. Skills cover general, context-independent knowledge, while competencies refer to experience-based and context-dependent knowledge (Gammelgaard and Larson, 2001). However, there is a lack of consensus and clarification on these skills and competencies or their grouping.

A plethora of skills and competencies are discussed in the literature from various perspectives (e.g., Dubey and Gunasekaran, 2015; Shou and Wang, 2017). This study reviewed several academic and industry articles to identify skills and competencies required for supply chain managers to manage their current and future supply chains and group them. While it may be argued that a host of other supply chain skills and competencies could be identified in the literature, no other items appeared most often in the recent literature as listed in the following pages:

Supply Chain Planning

Supply chain planning is critical for proactively managing supply chains. Therefore, supply chain managers are expected to move from a reactive mode to a planning mode. This includes location planning (APICS, 2009), production planning (Prajogo and Sohal, 2013; Shou and Wang, 2017), and distribution planning (Prajogo and Sohal, 2013), to determine the need for material and capacity to address expected demand and to efficiently distribute products among suppliers, manufacturing facilities, distribution centers, warehouses, and customers through a logistics network.

Supply Chain Functional Skills

Functional skills are those skills that relate to SCM functions. Supply chain managers are expected to demonstrate these skills and often form the basis of their job requirements. Yet, studies have highlighted that it is rare to find a supply chain manager with the breadth and depth of skills required to run a global supply chain (Tantham *et al.*, 2012). With supply chains becoming increasingly complex and global, supply chain managers must possess end-to-end SCM skills rather than focus on one or two functions such as warehousing or transportation. This starts with a solid understanding of relevant global and local policies and procedures and other regulatory requirements (Shou and Wang, 2017; Tantham *et al.*, 2017). Similarly, a solid understanding of supply chain processes is crucial for process management, which includes process mapping, integration, reengineering, and optimization (Mangan and Christopher, 2005; APICS, 2009), which allows supply chains to maintain required levels of service and enhance customer value (Ellinger and Ellinger, 2014). Supply chain financing skills are critical for reducing supply chain-wide costs and sustaining cash flow (Dubey and Gunasekaran, 2015; Tantham *et al.*, 2017). The other functional skills include strategic sourcing (APICS, 2009; Dubey and Gunasekaran, 2015); asset and inventory management (APICS, 2009; Tantham *et al.*, 2017); transportation management (Dubey and Gunasekaran, 2015; Tantham *et al.*, 2017); freight management (APICS, 2009); warehouse management (APICS, 2009; Dubey and Gunasekaran, 2015; Shou and Wang, 2017); and management of outsourcing activities to third-party logistics (3PL) companies (Prajogo and Sohal, 2013; Tantham *et al.*, 2017).

Supply Chain Technologies

Previous studies have reported the significance of supply chain managers' awareness and knowledge of a broad range of both internally focused and externally focused supply chain technologies (Prajogo and Sohal, 2013). For instance, using technologies in supply chains could bring operational benefits like cost reduction and service improvements and strategic benefits such as improvements in product planning and innovation (Prajogo and Sohal, 2013). This includes e-commerce technologies, enterprise resource planning (ERP) systems, and e-procurement tools such as e-auction and online bidding and tendering (Prajogo and Sohal, 2013). In addition, the recent advancement in information technology, robotics and automation, blockchain technology, artificial intelligence, and machine learning, and other Industry 4.0 technologies that are enabled by data, digital technologies, and automation (Hofmann *et al.*, 2019) implies that present and future supply chain managers must possess awareness and knowledge of these technologies to leverage the potential benefits of these technologies and enhance business competitiveness.

Software Application

Strong knowledge of various software applications is critical for supply chain managers to enhance their supply chain competitiveness (Gammelgaard and Larson, 2001; Shou and Wang, 2017). This is because recent years have witnessed tremendous growth in SCM software like warehouse management, transportation management systems, and supply chain planning and execution (Prajogo and Sohal, 2013).

Analytical Skills

Analytical skills involve quantitative and statistical skills, critical reasoning, and problem-solving (Gammelgaard and Larson, 2001). Studies have reported that supply chain managers must possess strong analytical skills such as data processing, demand forecasting, and performance evaluation (Myers *et al.*, 2004; Shou and Wang, 2017). Supply chain managers must possess the competency to apply mathematical and statistical models in collecting, analyzing, and interpreting quantitative data (APICS, 2009). In addition, supply chain managers must possess benchmarking skills and skills to scrutinize and break down facts and derive meaningful insights (APICS, 2009). The advent of the big data revolution implies that the significance of analytical skills will be even more significant in the future.

Supply Chain Sustainability

Clear awareness and knowledge of sustainable business practices (e.g., triple bottom line) are critical for supply chain managers (Prajogo and Sohal, 2013). This is because supply chains are considered a game-changer in the fight against climate change. For most companies, end-to-end supply chain emissions are much higher than the direct emissions from their own operations. According to McKinsey, a typical consumer company's supply chain accounts for more than 80% of greenhouse-gas emissions and more than 90% of the impact on air, land, water, biodiversity, and geological resources. By implementing a net-zero supply chain, companies can amplify their climate impact, enable emission reductions in hard-to-abate sectors, and accelerate climate action (BCG,

2021). To achieve this, supply chain managers must apply lean and six sigma management tools to identify and reduce or eliminate waste in all areas of a supply chain and reduce error (APICS, 2009; Prajogo and Sohal, 2013; Dubey and Gunasekaran, 2015). Similarly, supply chain managers must demonstrate the ISO 14001 standard, the most widely recognized environmental standard. It sets out the criteria for an environmental management system (Balasubramanian and Shukla, 2017). Similarly, supply chain managers must attempt to close the loop with reverse logistics such as take-back schemes and effective mechanisms for processing returns, contributing to the circular economy concept (APICS, 2009; Tantham *et al.*, 2017).

Leadership and Decision-making Skills

Leadership is arguably vital in any profession at middle and senior levels, and the supply chain is no exception (Shou and Wang, 2017). Supply chain managers must demonstrate strong leadership skills to effectively lead and manage diverse teams and impact competitive advantage through successfully implementing supply chain initiatives (Ellinger and Ellinger, 2014). In addition to leadership skills, sound decision-making skills is an important competency of supply chain managers (Gammelgaard and Larson, 2001; Prajogo and Sohal, 2013; Shou and Wang, 2017). Whilst economically, the cost of an ineffective decision and the value of an effective one can affect the bottom line of not only their own organization but also those of their supply chain partners (Tantham *et al.*, 2017). For instance, during COVID-19, the quality and timeliness of their supply chain decisions are critical.

General Management Skills

Several studies have stressed the importance of broader, general management skills for supply chain managers in order for them to be able to lead their supply chains, especially during turbulent times (Shou and Wang, 2017; Tatham *et al.*, 2017). This includes time management, project management, risk management, quality management, and change management (Gammelgaard and Larson, 2001; APICS, 2009; Shou and Wang, 2017; Tatham *et al.*, 2017).

Relationship Management Skills

Supply chain managers need to be equipped with the skills and knowledge to manage logistics and be relationship managers (Mangan and Christopher, 2005). As such, effective relationship management such as employee relationship, customer relationship, and supply relationship require good people skills and negotiation skills (Gammelgaard and Larson, 2001, APICS, 2009; Tantham *et al.*, 2017). In addition, supply chain managers must demonstrate the ability to manage in a sensible, fair, and efficient manner (APICS, 2009). Similarly, cross-functional collaboration is typically unstructured, informal communication that is dependent upon people's ability to trust each other and build meaningful relationships (Ellinger and Ellinger, 2014). There is a heightened need for supply chain managers to develop cross-functional collaboration (Gammelgaard and Larson, 2001; Mangan and Christopher, 2005). Further, supply chain managers must be strong team players who can work effectively in a matrix organization structure with cross-cultural, intra-, and inter-organization teams (Prajogo and Sohal, 2013; Shou and Wang, 2017). Further, in today's globalized supply chain, a host of cross-cultural issues arise from significant cultural differences from people in different regions (Shou and Wang, 2017). Supply chain managers, therefore, must possess cross-cultural management skills.

Soft Skills

Besides hard skills such as technological and analytical skills, supply chain managers need soft skills for effectively communicating and dealing with internal and external stakeholders (Shou and Wang, 2017; CIPS, 2019). This includes effective oral communication, written communication skills (Gammelgaard and Larson, 2001; Tantham *et al.*, 2017), and the ability to document, generate business reports, and report status to stakeholders (Shou and Wang, 2017).

Chapter 2

Interview with Supply Chain Experts and Leaders

Introduction

Interviewees were asked to identify potential changes that may impact on the skills and competency required by supply chain professionals in the future especially during COVID-19 pandemic. Some of the interview questions are listed below:

- What are the key goals and targets that you have set for your supply chain staff?
- What are the essential skills or competencies for decision-making for supply chain issues?
- Where do you see yourself in the next 5 years?
- Is there anything that you would like to add to be a competent supply chain manager during the pandemic?

Prior to the interviews, a list of prospective interviewees in various organizations was drawn up, and each of these interviewees was contacted via email inviting their participation in the interviews. The interviews were conducted on a one-to-one basis and averaged approximately 60 minutes. We have conducted interviews with 22 senior supply chain professionals and leaders from 6 countries in Asia to identify the skill competencies to be successful supply chain professionals. They are represented from the logistics industry, manufacturing industry, retailing industry, and e-commerce companies (See Appendix C for each company's overview). In addition, a secondary analysis of published information including interview data on Al-Futtaim Logistics was conducted to complement the primary interviews.

Secondary Analysis of Al-Futtaim Logistics from Dubai

Company Introduction

Established in the 1980s, Al-Futtaim Logistics is a leading regional provider of world-class supply chain solutions, with a global reach to 150 countries through its strategic alliance with international network partners (Al-Futtaim, 2022). The company has many years of specialized experience in several key sectors. It has a comprehensive understanding of the complexities involved in providing solutions for Automotive, Retail, Fashion, Food, Footwear, Industrial, Engineering, Electronics, High-Tech, Humanitarian, and Project Cargo. Al-Futtaim Logistics service capabilities extend to Freight Forwarding & Customs Clearance, Warehousing & Contract Logistics, Goods Transportation & Distribution, Corporate Transportation, Relocations, and International Moving (ICC UAE, 2022). The company manages over 250,000 square meters of warehousing and 1,000,000 square meters of open storage space. It has a fleet of 600, delivering services to blue-chip multinational companies in the automotive, retail, and other sectors. Its fleet and operational centers are strategically located at major air and sea hubs in the UAE (Al-Futtaim, 2022). With its full connectivity from strategically located state-of-the-art facilities at the region's most important freight hubs, Al-Futtaim Logistics offers a full range of advanced end to end SCM solutions such as (Al-Futtaim, 2022):

- Global Freight Forwarding and Local Services
- Warehousing and Contract Logistics
- Local and Cross Border Transportation and Distribution
- Corporate Transportation
- Domestic and International Relocations
- Finished Vehicle Distribution
- Lead Logistics and 4PL

While Al-Futtaim Logistics was able to create innovative solutions by leveraging sophisticated technology such as the use of drones in warehouses, big data analytics, machine learning (ML), and artificial intelligence (AI) platforms, it continues to focus and invest in learning and development to enhance employee skills and competencies, and want to attract, develop, and retain the best logistics expertise in the region. Al-Futtaim Logistics has annual personal development plans for each employee, which is linked to enhancing business performance.

Questions and Answers

What key goals and targets have the company set for their supply chain staff?

In the words of Dr. Raman Kumar, Managing Director of Al-Futtaim Logistics, "Initially, we had three main criteria that we wanted to achieve which included operational efficiency, increasing our customer satisfaction, and increasing employee engagement. Once we managed to achieve this, we looked at our business expansion and what additional value we can give to our customers" (Hotel & Catering News Middle east, 2021).

Al-Futtaim Logistics is constantly reevaluating the systems that they have put in place, identifying weaknesses in supply chains, and pushing the standards of reliability and efficiency ever higher so that it maintains its dominant position in the 3PL industry (The CEO Magazine, 2020). Further, Al Futtaim Logistics is looking to expand its areas of specialization beyond transportation to AI and cold storage, opening up opportunities to provide end-to-end supply chain services in an ever-widening array of sectors. For instance, Al Futtaim Logistics has launched a state-of-the-art cold storage facility in the Jebel Ali Free Zone with multiple temperature-controlled storage units, including world-class warehouse management and temperature monitoring system (The CEO Magazine, 2020).

Key goals for the supply chain department are to

- Early adoption of new technologies to offer custom solutions to customers and expand their footprint across the Middle East and North Africa
- Adopt sustainable freight practices to cut carbon emissions
- Deliver innovative and creative logistics solutions that customers value

One of Al-Futtaim Logistics' main and emerging focus areas is cold-chain logistics. According to their Managing Director, "Moving and storing temperature-sensitive packaged food and beverages requires continuous commitment and dedication to the highest quality standards" (mid-east information, 2021). Al-Futtaim Logistics' multi-temperature cold storage warehousing facility ranging from +18°C to –22°C has scalable space for the growing needs of their customers. It incorporates world-class warehouse management technology, including capturing all the attributes of the products combined with double-deep storage that optimizes space utilization and enables high throughput (Al-Futtaim, 2022).

What are the essential skills and competencies required for staff in meeting the goals and targets?

The essential skills and competencies for the company include

i. Listening to what the customer wants and translating high expectations into solutions.
ii. Demonstrating professionalism and commitment to meeting customer needs.
iii. Problem-solving skills are critical and will remain critical for the next 5 years, as we see many supply chain issues and bottlenecks that require complex problem-solving.

In addition, knowledge of the new technologies and the ability to continuously learn and develop new skills and competencies as per market trends is critical. Integrating digital technology and data is key to successful real-time acceleration of operations. In the words of the Managing Director, information is critical, and hence data analytics is vital for Al-Futtaim Logistics. The Managing Director wants the data analytics team to give the best results to the top management to make the necessary changes. For example, understanding customer behavior changes such as changes in ordering patterns allowed us to change the warehouse configuration so that fast-moving items could be placed in a better position to be picked up very quickly (Logistics ME, 2021).

Will these skills remain the same for the next 5 years? Why or why not?

Future success relies on leveraging data-driven operations. The know-how to leverage data is critical. This includes using data for predictive analysis, digitizing the process, integrating multiple touchpoints in the supply chain, proactive planning, and multi-supplier order visibility. The relevance is even more significant as e-commerce is accelerating at a fast pace. Technology will keep changing. Employees would need to adapt to the new changes in technology. Big data, AI, and ML are the future. This doesn't mean employees will be replaced, but the way they think needs to change, their thinking level needs to be higher (higher-order thinking) to understand what changes need to bring to the business and improve customer satisfaction. AI and ML will be helpful to identify patterns in this fast-changing environment. Whether it's utilizing chatbots or implementing bots to automate some of the routines, AI plays a part in the e-commerce world. It's possible to automate aspects of order processing and fulfillment, shipping, and invoicing with the help of AI and chatbots. This will allow staff to concentrate on other areas, such as customer service.

Even though technology will change the way we operate, the CEO of Al-Futtaim logistics believes that their workers too will adapt to the latest technology. Employees need to learn to work with machines and robots, especially at the warehouse. Automation of warehouse operations has accelerated now. According to their General Manager, "We see that the digitization of fulfillment centers will be the next area of focus. At Al-Futtaim Logistics, we are trying to see how to automate our processes that will help to reduce repetitive tasks, and how we can move information from one system to another with efficient integration." Al-Futtaim Logistics is working to see how they can do inventory counts with multiple cycle counts in the fulfillment center, using drone and RFID technology. The ultimate goal is to move quickly through the supply chain to get the product to our end consumer (Logistics ME, 2021).

The next 5 years will present a significant opportunity in the Food and Beverage Sector (F&B). According to the Dubai Chamber of Commerce and Industry & Euromonitor analysis, online sales within the UAE's food and beverage market surged 255% year-over-year in 2020 to reach $412 million (Dubai Chamber of Commerce, 2021). The study predicted the value of online food and beverage sales in the country to reach $619 million by 2025 and record a compound annual growth (CAGR) of 8.5% over the 2020–2025 period. Moreover, the F&B market segment has high demand, and depending on the type of product, on-time fulfillment can be an essential competitive advantage. According to Binoy George, General Manager, Warehousing, and Last Mile distribution at Al-Futtaim Logistics, "Today, we see those customers with premium products with shorter shelf-life and quicker turnaround to the retailers or direct consumer." To seize this growth opportunity, Al-Futtaim Logistics has launched new service offerings such as the cold store for food & beverages (F&B) sector and last-mile delivery (B2C). The temperature within the facility itself is one of the most important factors to maintain for F&B products. A slight temperature change would dull the freshness of the products and demonstrate the importance of keeping the temperature consistent from the warehouse to the end consumer (Hotel & Catering News Middle East, 2021). In the words of their General Manager, "One of the most critical features and challenges is maintaining the temperature across the whole chain." This is because the supply chain has multiple touchpoints right from the product of origin with the proper packaging and static temperature to be moved into the transport unit, which also needs to be at the right temperature moving it into the destination port, first-mile and into the temperature-controlled storage facilities (Hotel & Catering News Middle East, 2021).

In addition to cold-chain facilities, better warehouse management is critical for the F&B sector. Fast-moving goods are now placed in a better position for efficiency and pick up as customers in the F&B segment are looking for same-day delivery.

Is there any special skill or competency that supply chain professionals should develop during the pandemic? Please elaborate.

Digital platforms are critical for driving business growth, requiring digital transformation across all verticals. The sales team and logistics teams have to work closely. Al-Futtaim Logistics has implemented the Sales Product Management platform, enabling the customer order to be picked up quickly. Increasing digital retail and e-commerce has increased the logistics volume. But the time frame was reduced. The grocery retail sector is a big business opportunity but low value but higher volume. Fresh food and pantry products have increased during the pandemic. Last-mile home delivery increased. Order fulfillment in a few hours is required. This requires digital technologies. Employees need to use technology to drive business operations.

Al-Futtaim Logistics was able to identify critical opportunities for their business to grow. According to their Managing Director, "The pandemic has created a new opportunity — the most prominent being technology. Previously, we talked about four days or even 7-day delivery; now, we are talking about same-day delivery or 3-to 4-hour delivery. E-commerce and digital order management have accelerated during the pandemic. Supply chain professionals need to be dynamic to make the supply chain agile (Logistics ME, 2021).

Al-Futtaim Logistics has rolled out a yard management system for vehicles and new tech for contract logistics, fragile transport, and last-mile delivery. It has enabled the customer to see the flow of the goods or order throughout the supply chain (Logistics & Transport Middle East, 2021). In the words of Binoy George, General Manager – Warehousing, Al Futtaim Logistics: "Our adaptations to the E-commerce digital momentum and adaptability to changing consumer preferences in the F&B logistics sector has ensured sustainable growth and the expansion of its services from the UAE, to KSA and Oman" (mid-east information, 2021).

The ongoing pandemic didn't seem to deter Al-Futtaim Logistics regarding their business operations. Quick and adaptable changes were made and this was at the forefront of the company's plans. In the words of their Managing Director, Dr. Raman Kumar, "At Al-Futtaim Logistics, we had a strong business continuity plan in place which allowed us to manage the crisis." He also mentioned, "The biggest challenge we saw was the mindset of our customers, especially when it came to delivery services and the steps that would need to be taken to ensure that everyone was safe. We had to implement a new HSE strategy and follow strict protocols to ensure that everyone would be protected during our services" (Hotel & Catering News Middle East, 2021).

Further, Al-Futtaim Logistics won the "Hero of the Pandemic Award" in the fulfillment category at the Transport & Logistics Middle East awards. During the pandemic, Al-Futtaim Logistics nearly quadrupled the order fulfillment volumes while maintaining 99.8% order accuracy for its third-party customers, with a turnaround time (TAT) adherence of 98.7%. The company is scaling up its services to meet the needs of e-commerce and marketplace clients with all-inclusive last-mile home delivery solutions (Al-Futtaim, 2022).

Conclusion

The secondary case study of Al-Futtaim Logistics has provided significant insights on the focus of logistics providers now and in the next five years. It showed the importance of technology and employees to work hand in hand to achieve business success. The study also shows that while the COVID-19 pandemic has created significant disruptions and challenges, it has also made significant opportunities. Employees need to upskill and reskill themselves to stay relevant and competitive.

References

Al-Futtaim (2022). About Al-Futtaim Logistics. https://www.aflogistics.com/about-us/.

ICC UAE (2022). Al Futtaim Logistics Company LLC — ICC UAE. https://iccuae.com/0108.html.

Hotel & Catering News Middle East (2021). The Big Chill, Cold Chain Fulfilment. https://www.hotelnewsme.com/hotel-news-me/the-big-chill-cold-chain-fulfilment/.

The CEO Magazine (2020). Remarkably fast: Raman Kumar. https://www.theceomagazine.com/executive-interviews/transportation-logistics/raman-kumar/.

Mid-east information (2021). Al-Futtaim Logistics Wins Cold Chain Service Provider of the Year Award. https://mid-east.info/al-futtaim-logistics-wins-cold-chain-service-provider-of-the-year-award/.

Logistics ME (2021). In conversation with Dr. Raman Kumar, Managing Director at Al-Futtaim Logistics. https://www.youtube.com/watch?v=-JQ0XC9AQMMQ.

Interview with Mega Group (MG): A Retail Giant in India

Company Introduction

Started by first-generation entrepreneur, Mega Group (MG) is a retail giant in India with its scale of operations captured by the quote:

> *On any given day, more than 2 million people visit our stores and digital networks, experience our product brands...*

With the simple idea of retaining Indian value in its business, the MG operates brands in food, fast moving consumer goods, and fashion through its over 1,000 stores covering a quarter million square feet across 300 plus cities in India. Millions more interact through its ecommerce, social media, and multiple electronic wallets. Its supply chain's biggest challenge is running its perishable food value chain connecting small towns and cities. It owns around 10 own brands in food. In fashion it handles international brands like Lee Cooper and John Miller, besides a number of its own brands.

Supply Chain Challenges

Over time besides operating with the large format multi-brand stores, MG has entered in small format (500–3,000 square feet) business with multiple brands — all food supply chain. It employs over 30,000 people to run its different businesses. Together with this, it has increased its presence in online sales through e-commerce.

The goals of supply chain, particularly in the small format food chains, being to operate within budget targets, focus on revenues while maintaining supplies in the shelfs and freshness of perishable products; keep items in pipeline but fresh at store. This challenged decision on volumes of supplies in future, number and location of new warehouses besides their size, vehicle fleet size, and so on. Maintaining a fleet of over 200 trucks following COVID-19 protocols while moving inventory across the country and trying to optimize fuel utilization, given rising fuel price, were the biggest challenges facing the supply chain personnel. As government policy required shifting from a VAT system to a GST system, accounting for goods movement became critical.

The supply chain challenges were severe in items like furniture and electronics with pan India demand now being met by limited local sources giving higher discounts to fill the gap left due to interrupted supplies from China. On the other hand, in food price there were limited margins and so major discounts could not be given while maintaining fresh supplies. These items therefore required local purchase near the MG stores demanding local/regional warehousing that catered to a cluster of stores and supplies from surrounding villages. On the other hand, general merchandise and fashion items with higher margins and bulk supplies from central warehouses/mother warehouse needed volume logistics/full truck load to maximize sale and profits. Together with this was added the omnichannel approach of customers ordering online to be delivered at doorstep (using 3PL provider) or be picked up by customer at nearest MG store. Catalogs for online purchase were customized by both local zip code as also nearest store stocking although as much as 90% stocks were common across MG stores. Most of such activities were complicated by uncertainties of supply and demand due to unpredictable customer behavior in the times of SARS and COVID-19.

Questions and Answers

What are the essential skills or competencies for decision-making for supply chain issues?

For the complexities of supply chain, personnel skills in areas of optimized inventory management were critical. With the added uncertainties of COVID-19 this required a two-tiered skill demonstration. At the level of warehouse, it required use of software and data to handle two different supply chain models — one relatively centralized, long lead time bulk inventory management of general merchandise and fashion items and the other of a more decentralized, small-sized local supply chains for perishable products. Omnichannels for both these items needed to be maintained as 3PL members tried to meet online customer demands locally for both type of items and so aimed for zero stock out at store shelves as an important KPI for staff. On the other hand, there was uncertainty of supplies due to COVID-19 lockdown/slow down as also unpredictable order mix, order size, and order location on customer side due to less frequent and higher volume buying, particularly of perishables to avoid frequent contact, possibility of local outbreak of pandemic. This demanded accurate forecasting of demand and supply to run the business efficiently and profitably under supplier and customer threat of low switching cost of shifting from one eCommerce company to another.

Specific skills required at operations level in warehouses included use of WMS for optimum lot size, fulfillment, and expiry management. This included know analysis, inventory management to avoid empty shelf, particularly with increased volatility of online orders and drop in regular in-store purchase due to pandemic. It required revised bigger lot size for fast-moving items and flagging for priority pick-up and delivery of such items. In spite of this, some customer orders could not be met in pandemic uncertainty of supplies, needing substitutes to be proposed or refunds to be made to customers. Inventory management was done using SAP and had not shifted to a cloud-based system. With critical skills in managing inventory, most warehouse employees using Excel-based systems were graduates with 2–3 years of relevant experience and underwent regular refresher courses to update their skills.

On the other hand, most senior managers working on SAP needed different mindsets to face long-term challenges. Senior managers sitting at HQ had technical qualification — mechanical or production engineering preferably with an MBA. By being forward thinking SAP could give efficient outputs as quality and robust inputs were provided by managers. Periodic training on analytics and other SAP advances were given to such managers to improve forecasting models used.

Besides RFID, the use of technology for both market penetration and also convenience had to be mobile phone apps and not so much computers or laptops due to poor Internet connectivity and user knowledge in remote areas. Dark rooms or special storage space and manpower needed to be created in MG stores for online order assembly and distribution both for 3PL delivery and customer pick up from store. Generally, mobile phone-based OTP was used to verify orders and deliver.

Where do you see yourself in the next 5 years?

The next 2–3 years MG needs to focus on consolidating warehouse and infrastructure to reduce transit time to be able to increase availability for customers while also reducing cost as road infrastructure improved and government-controlled fuel price increase. This included skills to reduce costs of defect/fulfillment error and optimize management of rural infrastructure (change the current 30–40% sourcing directly from farmers to 60–70%) as most competitors were sourcing 60–70% from farmers under their "farm to fork" program. With help of technology, output per capita of employees needed to be increased without increasing manpower (e.g., one person throughput of 10 cartons per day to increase by 1.5 times) based on changes process and technology. This was a challenge as different geographies in India had different levels of productivity (East of India productivity lower than North India). Lot of gap to bridge in all this without increasing cost using planning, technology, and accurate forecasting was required to maintain competitiveness in supply chain. The company was using technology and forecasting to do cross-docking for better utilization of warehouse space.

Is there anything that you would like to add to be a competent supply chain manager during the pandemic?

According to a company senior management, supply chain was a constraint during the pandemic and was likely to continue post-pandemic due to reduction in manpower at warehouse, although throughput was likely to reach pre-pandemic levels. Different ways to visualize constraints — for example, this needed reduction in process steps from say 10 to 8 to increase productivity by say 10%. Senior supply chain managers were working with process data for this. Multi-skilling of staff to keep operations going by working extra time if some teams contracted the pandemic and standby pool of drivers and 3PL service providers was created for uninterrupted supplies. However, all this increased the cost of supply chain and logistics for MG during the pandemic as the priority was on meeting customer orders as far as possible.

For improvement at company end, better production, inventory management at supplier end was necessary through suitable vendor development skills to be inculcated in MG staff. For example, food items had to be 100% scanned at supplier end, and apparel packs color coded with size (XXL/XL, etc.) in a particular color pack to avoid break bulking to speed up cross-docking; 50–60% sorting after break bulking was currently done by MG not suppliers. Pre-pandemic mindset changed with food items cross docked and sent to MG store shelves as customers did not come back for the items every day during the pandemic and a large volume sale could be lost from empty shelves.

In future, vendor development efforts had to be extended to tier-II and III suppliers. This needed developing vendor management portal to link with such suppliers. This would help MG keep promise of servicing eCommerce clients in metros within 2–3 km radius of its stores in 2 hours. In future, this would promote more online B2C business in tier-II and III cities and towns, raising the challenge of bringing seamless link with small local suppliers of perishables like vegetables and dairy products in remote areas. In future, the supply chain might need to have capacity to service 10,000 plus outlets and their B2C clients of a collaborating partner with many of these customers operating on membership basis.

Conclusion

In nationwide retail chains spread across large geographic area in India, the challenge was primarily of inventory management. With each store stocking both general merchandise and fashion items with bulk handling from centralized warehouses and perishable products from local supplies close to cluster of stores, using regional warehousing, this challenge was more complex. To this was added challenges of omni channel demands of eCommerce in the wake of pandemic when customers wanted to stock at home by buying bulk and infrequently. For business challenge was in fulfillment, reducing stock out while optimizing cost. On the other hand, supplies were uncertain and less than order quantities. This resulted in critical inventory management challenges at warehouses and complex forecasting at HQ and zonal office levels. Besides buffer stock, standby human resources were needed, all adding to cost of business. With the pandemic, a learning opportunity in inventory cross-docking and working with lower human resources, processes needed to be modified/developed for more robust systems going into the future to institutionalize the learnings from the pandemic. Tiered supplier inventory management required to be seamlessly integrated to increase the reach of retail chains into tier-II and III towns and rural areas.

Interview with Chief Operations Officer of ChiliBeli in Indonesia

Company Introduction

Chilibeli is an online shopping application for daily products such as fruit, vegetables, basic necessities, and other household needs that carries the concept of social commerce — buying and selling activities that involve social interaction between users in a community through online and offline social networks.

Products from farmers and producers of fast moving consumer goods will be connected directly to Chilibeli Partners, whose role is to make it easier for people around them to shop easily to get quality fresh products in an environment.

Besides being able to make it easier for people in the surrounding environment, Chilibeli Partners can get extra income or additional spending money from every transaction for each member of their community, with the flexibility to manage time for other things.

Chilibeli customers can be divided into two segments, namely members and community leaders. Members are users who can directly buy products through the community leader who we call Chilibeli Friends to manage member spending in exchange for commissions.

Questions and Answers

What are the key goals and targets that you have set for your supply chain staff?

Key goals for the supply chain department are to

- Ensure good service with on time delivery
- Manage cost to ensure efficiency

Since most of the products are perishable, it is important to deliver the products on time to ensure freshness with proper packaging to protect against contamination. This requires a lot of coordination among the farmers, community leaders, and the members of Chilibeli. The day the orders are taken, the customers will receive the delivery by 5 pm the next day. This is a commitment to the buyers and it is critical that this policy is maintained consistently.

Thus, the key measurements for the supply chain department are

- Ensure product quality — Products are fresh upon delivery
- On time delivery — Delivered by 5 pm the next day for orders taken today
- Proper packaging — Products are well protected by packaging

What are the essential skills and competencies for staff in meeting the goals and targets?

In order to achieve the key measurements, Damon the COO has developed processes, policies, and people skills to reach these goals. Processes are continuously reviewed and improved to meet the goals. Last mile delivery is one of the challenging processes especially for rural areas. The company needs to coordinate closely with the community leaders in those rural areas to deliver the products as some of the residents do not have a proper postal address. This situation is worsened since communication is limited since some of these customers are not using social media.

In terms of people skill sets, system thinking is critical so that the staff can see the whole end-to-end process and not work in silo. Coordination with the partners and teamwork are also important to ensure the delivery can be completed by 5 pm the next day. As Indonesia is made up of many islands, it requires more coordination to ensure the products are delivered to the customers via multi-model transportation.

Data are exploding and Chilibeli makes use of data to better understand their customers and how to reach them in the digital marketplace. They also need to optimize supply chains, improve operations, and manage various facilities to be profitable. That's where data analytics comes in. Many organizations are struggling with more data than they know what to do with. Experts in data analytics can take that information and uncover new insights businesses are missing. As more companies now rely on data to inform their business decisions, the demand for data analytics roles in e-commerce has accelerated. Data analytics will remain one of the most in-demand skills in coming years for their staff, as the analysis of consumer behavior and internal infrastructure data continue to be improved and enhanced through AI augmentation. Based on the data collected for each transaction, the supply chain team are able to make better decision to plan and deliver their goods to the customers on time. They are trained in using business analytics software to assist them in forecasting sales and scheduling delivery.

Lastly, soft skills are essential for their staff to build better relationship with their stakeholders. The soft skills required for SCM include excellent communication skills, leadership, time management, negotiating, and problem-solving skills. Soft skills are harder to characterize. They're things like personality traits and interpersonal skills. Soft skills can make or break a conversation and are strongly related to customer service skills. Why? Because to deliver high customer service level, communication and interpersonal skills are vital. To carry out a retail job effectively, it's also important to talk clearly, and be patient, empathetic, and friendly according to Damon.

Do you still see these skills are still the same for the next five years? Why or why not? Please elaborate.

Leverage on data becoming critical as e-commerce is accelerating at a fast pace. AI and ML may be useful to identify patterns in this fast-changing environment. Whether it's utilizing chatbots or implementing bots to automate some of the routines, AI has a part to play in the ecommerce world. It's possible to automate parts of order processing and fulfillment, shipping, and invoicing with the help of AI and chatbots. This will allow staff to concentrate on other areas, such as customer service.

Is there any special skills or competency that supply chain professionals should develop during the pandemic? Please elaborate.

Reacting quickly to disruption requires a flexible ecosystem of suppliers and partners that can handle sudden shortfalls or even produce new products. That means setting up alternative sourcing and making the most of technologies to optimize cost, improve visibility across the network, and accelerate reaction times. Those dependent on imports are shifting inward or closer to their core markets. As for Chilibeli, they are fortunate to be able to source their products within Indonesia. Amid the COVID-19 pandemic, the company needs greater visibility into the supply chains of their suppliers. More companies are applying automation and robotics to make their supply chain more autonomous and adding suppliers in their home markets to ensure business continuity. Control tower solutions that integrate data across the entire supply chain, 5G technology, and blockchain offer supply chain team real-time visibility. Companies can better calibrate supply with forecast demand by comparing internal capacity data with real-time demand signals such as weather data.

In fact, building resilient supply chain increases the costs of operations according to Damon. Instead of using a centralized warehouse, they have split the storage into a few warehouses. This will avoid a situation where some of the staff in a warehouse are infected with COVID-19 and the warehouse needs to be shutdown. By decentralizing the warehouses, each warehouse can still operate independently without being lockdown completely.

Similarly, the drivers employed to deliver the goods to customers are split into a few teams. They worked in different shifts and are not allowed to intermingle with each other. This will reduce the risk of spreading anyone infected with COVID-19 to another team affecting the delivery capacity. The company has also hired part-time drivers as the number of deliveries increased during the pandemic.

"In this pandemic period, we are not able to optimize our resources but to ensure our business continue with less disruption," said Damon.

Conclusion

As most of the products from Chilibeli are perishable, it is important to deliver the products on time to ensure freshness with proper packaging to protect against contamination. This requires a lot of coordination among the farmers, community leaders, and the members of Chilibeli. The day the orders are taken, the customers will receive the delivery by 5 pm the next day. Thus, the main goal of the company is to align their processes and resources to ensure on time delivery. The supply chain staff thus need to be able to have good people skills for coordination with stakeholders, soft skills to build relationship with their customers, and be analytical using the data from the system. And with the pandemic, additional skills are need to ensure their business is least disrupted. This in result in additional costs to increase the number of drivers and the number of warehouses. Last but not least, the adoption of technologies is accelerated during the pandemic to allow staff to work from home and customers to place orders online. The landscape of the supply chain will also be different as sourcing is done within the country instead of global sourcing for the cheapest products.

Interview with Dato Nachiappan Suppiah of Sitics Logistics Solutions from Malaysia

Company Introduction

Sikander and Haridas founded Sitics Logistic Solutions Pvt. Ltd. in 2007 intending to provide consumers and employees with logistics services that uphold the highest ethical standards. Sitics were offering services to a few corporates including MNCs by providing solutions and taking over several contracts. Currently, Sitics has grown to over

4,700 personnel, adding capabilities in warehousing, transportation, and becoming one of the first movers into the last-mile delivery area. Additionally, Sitics was able to sign up with the top e-commerce companies and have been enhanced by the use of technology to promote efficiencies and visibility, making it a win–win situation for both the company and the customer. Today, Sitics provides a full range of 3PL services and has grown to become one of India's leading logistics company's specializing in end-to-end SCM. Sitics has also expanded its services, in South India, across India, subsidiary in Malaysia, and recruited a joint venture partner in Thailand. Malaysia is a stepping stone into the APAC market, and Sitics has already secured business from major customers such as Mercedes Benz and Continental Tyres. Sitics is well-positioned to capitalize on its blistering growth rate of 40% year over year to become one of the leading logistics companies.

Questions and Answers

What are the key goals and targets that you have set for your supply chain staff?

Every country's economy relies heavily on logistics and SCM. A professional logistician in logistics and supply chain, like any other type of business, is crucial to the sector's success. This is because logistics is critical in abetting any country's economic growth (Khan *et al.*, 2020). Malaysia's logistics industry was valued at USD 37.60 billion in 2020, and it is expected to reach USD 55 billion by 2026, at a CAGR of more than 4% (Mordor Intelligence, 2022). Malaysia was also ranked among the top 10 countries in the world for the logistics sector (MIDA, 2021). As the logistics industry grows around the world, there is a concern about producing qualified logisticians to ensure this sector continues to contribute to the economy. In line with current needs, Malaysia has resolved to focus on the logistics sector as part of its plans to face global challenges. Thus, in the recent Twelfth Malaysia Plan, 2021–2025 (the RMK12) and National Fourth Industrial Revolution Policy (the 4IR Policy), the government has addressed the urge to develop competent human resources with the necessary knowledge and skills in the logistics sector. To achieve a competitive advantage, logistics companies must have well-trained, knowledgeable, and professional logisticians. It is important for the logisticians to be multitalented in terms of knowledge, skills, and competencies toward achieving the company's competitive advantage (Herden, 2019).

In an interview with logistics experts, Dato Nachiappan Suppiah, the Director of Sitics Logistic Solutions, emphasized four critical aims for logistics companies to be competitive namely cost reduction, process optimization, reliability, and the ability to stretch the resilient. To attain that, in today's competitive industry, increasing customer experience is overtaking service quality as a top goal for logisticians. Customer experience is a connection between a customer and a service or product, company, or any other aspect of the company that causes a customer to react and make a decision. This is a highly personal experience that involves the customer's participation at several stages, including physical, cognitive, emotional, affective, and social responses. Given the complexity of the customer experience, it's critical to provide solutions through technological advancement to inspire customers to be delighted (Pekovic and Rolland, 2020). Furthermore, the sustainable supplier is significant since it considers as a tool to identify improvement possibilities for the company's performance. Supplier selection is critical in assisting companies in achieving optimum ecological and economic benefits. From an industrial aspect, managing supplier selection criteria and processes implementation are critical to a company's acceptability and public image. Five criteria of a sustainable supplier evaluation are based on financial performance, service quality, technology, social responsibility, organization, and environmental skills (Luthra *et al.*, 2017). Alike, the ability to stay competitive requires both inspiration and the ability to acquire competencies. Teamwork, conflict management, leadership, and negotiation skills are among the examples of people skills that are required in every logistician. Rather than investing just in technology and processes, people play an important role in driving supply chain innovation (Wu *et al.*, 2018). Thus, increased customer happiness and value, as well as improved company's responsiveness, are all advantages of successful logisticians.

What are the essential skills or competencies for decision-making for supply chain issues?

As business environments develop at a quick pace, logistics sectors confront numerous issues. One of them is the critical need for logistics professionals who are well-trained and skilled. For example, customers have become acclimated to online shopping due to the COVID-19. Thus, the logistics sector is focussing on last-mile delivery services as a result of the consumer behavior revolution. Hence, logistics companies are essential to strengthen their last-mile competencies to keep up with the changes. The COVID-19 compelled the logistics industry to reevaluate and re-strategize the entire logistics operations so that it in line with the era of digitization (Pekovic and Rolland, 2020). As logistics practitioners seek to adjust to unstable and competitive business settings, managing the logistics and supply chain has grown increasingly difficult. The paradox of attaining cost reductions while increasing and improving customer service levels and enhancing supplier relationships throughout the supply chain processes adds to the complexity. One question that arises is what knowledge and skills logistics professionals require in order to face the broader requirements of their work in a globalized economy. As emphasized earlier, logistics practitioners should be multitalented predominantly in management skills in addition to having a breadth of specialist logistical knowledge and skills.

According to Dato Nachiapan, there are four primary abilities that logistics professionals should possess. The first step is to comprehend the marketplace or business environment. Due to the digital transformation, more collaborative operating models, greater efficiency, and shift in customer expectations have reshaped the marketplace. Hence, it is critical to learn about customers' needs, current product or service availability, customer satisfaction level with current products or services offered, as well as to develop a long-term relationship with both customers and suppliers. Understanding the marketplace or business environment is critical due to shifting customer expectations, technology developments, new competitors in the industry, and new ways to compete or cooperate (Herden, 2019). As a result, developing a supply chain process mapping or integration is critical. Mapping or integration refers to the process of gathering information about stakeholders in order to generate a global map of a company's supply chain. It simplifies data storage, enhances data analysis, and data can be stored in a single platform. This will assist businesses in examining a critical aspect of their operations at any stage of product design, manufacturing, and delivery.

Second, being customer-driven is an important ability in developing a customer-focused culture. It is critical to operating as a team to provide a positive client experience and achieve a better level of customer satisfaction. Customer engagement, responsiveness, breaking down team silos, technological advancement adoption, and customer loyalty rewards are just a few of the strategies that can aid logistics companies to exceed their customers' expectations. Companies can build relationships by recognizing and aiming for consumers based on their loyalty and tailoring offerings to meet their requirements (Wu *et al.*, 2018). Good oral communication skills, on the other hand, can make a big impact on overall logistical operations. Communication is crucial to supply chain success, nonetheless, it is also one of the least explored areas. It is impossible to overestimate the value of communication with internal and external stakeholders. By captivating the precise steps and implementing the required changes, it is possible to turn poor communication into overall logistics success. Comparable, better communication among stakeholders will bring more new ideas, which will develop the overall logistics process. Communication should always be a top focus in soft skills development, as it is crucial for creating and managing strong connections.

Third, is the capacity to stretch the resilience. This is the company's ability to adapt to adversity. When a crisis impairs a company's operations, such as the COVID-19 pandemic, business resilience is described as the ability for the company to survive, recover, and expand. It's the capability of a company to prepare the necessary and adapt to unexpected events. It is also how quickly the companies may fine-tune to a swift disruptive fluctuation that has a negative effect on the overall company's performance so that companies are able to continue functioning during a disruption. Supply chain resilience is also referred to as the form of how quickly companies recover to the pre-disruptive stage or a more desirable stage.

As the business landscape is dynamically and unpredictably growing, resilience is becoming progressively imperative (Sawyerr and Harrison, 2020). Thus, logistics professionals must continually seek advantage in adversity, look ahead, be flexible, and foster stakeholder engagement as some of the strategies to rethink the current business models toward generating sophisticated systemic resilience. Furthermore, supply chains must be able to identify, respond to, and recover from fluctuating situations. Supply chain integration, transparency, visibility, stakeholder participation, and good demand planning processes are also required.

Last but not least, building supply chain competencies is an important skill for logisticians to have in order to stay competitive. The supply chain function is always changing, and properly managing it is not easy. Given the challenges of the global supply chain, logistics professionals should never stop learning new skills and honing old ones. Capacity planning, order processing, demand management, logistics management, inventory management and optimization, warehousing and distribution, and continuous knowledge improvement procedures or methods are some of the abilities that logistics professionals must master and consistently develop. To succeed, today's logistics professionals rely on new core capabilities and enhanced industry knowledge. To be competitive, the logistics profession must constantly upskill and reskill its skills and competencies (Wahab *et al.*, 2021). People skills, adaptability, strong negotiating skills, critical crisis management abilities, cohesion skills, and team orientation are undoubtedly among the important qualities that current and future logisticians required.

Conclusion

Malaysia is on the verge of entering the Fourth Industrial Revolution (4IR). Smart manufacturing, integrated industry, and industrial internet are all terms used to describe 4IR (Hofmann and Rüsch, 2017). As technology advances, the logistics sector in Malaysia faces issues in terms of producing competent professionals particularly well-rounded professionals with a deep understanding of logistics operations. To manage the rising customer demand, it is critical to hire qualified logisticians (RMK12 & 4IR Policy). Failure to provide adequate and competent logistics professionals will stifle a country's economic growth. Hence, competence is crucial in assuring a logistician's productivity. With the increased recognition of logistics as a significant business concern, it is vital for logisticians to obtain suitable management skills and competencies. Alike, theory and practical knowledge and skills are seen as critical aspects for logistics professionals to remain competitive in the twenty-first century.

Interview with Managing Director of SCG Logistics and SCG Skills Development School in Thailand

Company Introduction

The interviewee is also the GMS Freight Transport Association (GMS Freta) chairman. GMS Freta is a regional coalition of freight and logistics association and companies in GMS Subregion. It consists of five countries which including Cambodia, Laos PDR, Myanmar, Thailand, and Vietnam. SCG Logistics is a subsidiary company under Siam Cement Group (SCG), the biggest Cement-building materials, chemicals, and packaging business in Thailand. SCG Logistics services cover inland, multimodal transport, warehousing, and fulfillment for B2B, C2C, and e-commerce sector. The company's vision is to become the most dominant 3PL with the strongest and largest network coverage in Thailand and GMS Countries.

Questions and Answers

What are the key goals and targets that you have set for your supply chain staff?

The key goals for freight and logistics company are to provide customer satisfaction by delivering the right product to the right place and the right customer at the right time. Logistics activities are not only transportation but also include warehousing, import, and export. Thus, to build a quality service, key target for company is to enhance customer predetermined target, which includes costs, quality, and service. We also have to make sure that our service can support customer operations to minimize their total supply chain costs.

Deploy KPIs (key performance indicator) for freight and logistics company in each department related to the above target are including:

- Minimize total cost;
- Shortening operations lead time (shortening order to cash cycle time);
- Lower inventory turnover; and
- Maximize forecasting accuracy (department plan to align with corporate master plan)

Challenges Due to Digital Disruption and Pandemic

Freight and logistics sector has been facing challenges from digital disruption. Moreover, pandemic has created more volatility, uncertainty, complexity, and ambiguity to the industry. Apart from that, it has been observed impact of technological upgrading requirements and operational management in this sector recently such as the adoption of AI and ML, Blockchain, and Automated Warehouse, which will change supply chain design to the new paradigm. In addition, COVID-19 has accelerated the adoption of new technology in Freight and Logistics sector while reshaping supply chain strategies to be more flexible, agile, and resilient (McKinsey & Company, 2020). Therefore, in the near future, especially in the post pandemic, skill requirement for freight and logistics professional has to be changed to align and fulfill post pandemic and the new supply chain paradigm. Table 1 outlines the current supply chain design and strategies compared to the post-pandemic new supply chain design and strategic as analyzed by the interviewee.

What are the essential skills or competencies for decision-making for supply chain issues?

Logistics professional competencies are including set of skills and behaviors in meeting company's goal and target as defined above should include the following:

- **Critical thinking and the ability to solve complex problem.** The staff should be able to confront the problem creativity and has

Table 1: The current and post-pandemic supply chain design and strategies

Current (before pandemic) Supply Chain Design and Strategies "Focus on cost saving"	**Post-Pandemic Supply Chain Design and Strategies "Focus on resilient and robustness"**
Focus on cost saving by adopted following design and strategies: 1. Lean supply chain concept. 2. Offshore outsourcing 3. Single (or fewer) supply supplier 4. Centralized (large warehouse)	Focus on resilient and robustness by planning to apply following design and strategies: 1. Supply chain redundancy 2. Local or nearshore outsourcing 3. Multiple supplier 4. Decentralized and micro warehouse Sharing resources, facilities, and data with partners and suppliers will be another strategy for industry to lower costs mitigate future risk. Freight and logistics industry will adopt technology and automation along the supply chain to enhance operations efficiency ranging from warehouse operations such as such as automate warehouse, to more advance technology in transportation technology like AI, machine learning, and autonomous vehicle driving.

the task achieving mindset. They should be able to use data and information to create scenarios and measurements and appropriate process to solve the problem.

- **Communication skill.** This is including the language skills (e.g., proficiency in native language and international language such as English with appropriate business-oriented dialogue.
- **Team working and collaborations.** The ability to work as a team internal and external.
- **Information technology as a user.** They should be able to know how to utilize and develop digitize process.
- **Leadership.** Logistics manager should have a strong visible leadership to inspire team member to achieving their targets.
- **Responsible and professionalism.** It is important that logistics manager should have sufficient knowledge and skill to manage

their job. This is also including ethical acting in professional works. (Responsible to company, supplier, and customer.)

Is there anything that you would like to add to be a competent supply chain manager during the pandemic?

The six essential skills mentioned above are the core competencies for logistics and supply chain manager. However, for post-pandemic, there are some additional skills necessary for logistics and supply chain manager as follows.

- **The ability to foresight and create scenarios.** This skill will be important in the future especially now we are in a VUCA economy (V: Volatility, U: Uncertainty, C: Complexity, and A: Ambiguity). Logistics and supply chain manager should be able to do foresight and create scenarios together with action plans in each scenario. Each scenario and action plan should be actionable and be able to mitigate risk that happened unexpectedly.
- **Risk assessment and trade-offs.** Logistics and supply chain manager should have the ability to monitor risk and find solutions to minimized risks.
- **The ability to integrating facts and data and make decision based on utilizing data.** Logistics and supply chain manager should be able to make decision by using data analytics. Thus, they should have skills on several tools for data analytics. They should be able to utilizing these reports for managerial insights and decisions. Moreover, logistics and supply chain manager should know which technology should be adopted in order to enhance productivity and efficiency in which operations.
- **The ability to create networks and close collaborations.** Future business need a strong network and collaborations especially for SCM. Logistics and supply chain manager should be able to build closed collaborations with different partners to support company's operations especially when company is facing a difficult situation such as unexpected disruptions.
- **Mindset in green and sustainability**. SC manager have to make sure that strategies they are created are meeting SDG goals. Thus,

they should have mindset in green and sustainability in doing business.

It can be seen that the previous supply chain (before pandemic) was focus on cost saving thus supply chain strategies such as lean management has been adopted. In terms of purchasing, offshore sourcing, single supplier, and centralized warehouse are key strategies for company. The challenges for global supply chain for post pandemic are how to make their supply chain more resilient while still competitive. Therefore, to meet that challenges risk mitigation must take into account on supply chain design and strategies as an addition to costs. In some cases, it may need to trading offs between costs and risks.

As explained in Table 1 that post-pandemic supply chain will focus more on resiliency, thus supply chain strategies will shift from cost saving to redundancy by having multiple suppliers from local or nearshore outsourcing with micro, decentralized warehouse for risk mitigation.

In addition to that, supply chain new paradigm, partnership, and closed collaborations with suppliers and customers are vital. Sharing resources, facilities, and data with partners and suppliers will be another strategy for industry to lower costs mitigate future risk. The adoption of new technology is inevitable in the industry to enhance operations efficiency ranging from warehouse operations such as automate warehouse, to more advance technology in transportation technology like AI, ML, and autonomous vehicle driving.

Interview with Mr. Ho Linh Phuoc, 3PL Director, Tiki Now Smart Logistics (TNSL) in Vietnam

Company Introduction

Tiki (abbreviation for "Tìm kiếm & Tiết kiệm," which means "Search & Save") is the fastest and most trusted B2C e-commerce platform in Vietnam. Tiki is well-known for its unique TikiNow service (2-hour delivery), world-class customer service with a 80+ NPS score, and diverse categories of 100% authentic products. Tiki is an all-in-one commercial ecosystem, consisting of member companies such as:

- Ti Ki Joint Stock Company ("TiKi") is the unit that establishes and organizes the e-commerce platform www.tiki.vn so that sellers can conduct part or the whole process of buying and selling goods, services on the e-commerce platform.
- Tikinow Smart Logistics Co., Ltd. ("TNSL") is a provider of end-to-end logistics services, transportation services, postal services for E-commerce platform www.tiki.vn. TikiNow Smart Logistics, established in September 2019, will be responsible for all of Tiki's forwarding activities and may provide B2C, B2B2C transportation services for other businesses. TikiNow Smart Logistics currently owns a system of operation centers with a total area of over 70,000 square meter nationwide. Services of TikiNOW Smart Logistics include warehousing and order processing services; shipping services.
- Ti Ki Trading Company Limited ("Tiki Trading") is a unit that sells goods and services on the e-commerce platform.
- Retail unit Tiki Trading and Exchange offer 10 million products from 26 categories serving millions of customers nationwide.

With the motto "All for Customers," Tiki always strives to improve the quality of services and products, thereby bringing a complete shopping experience to Vietnamese customers with fast delivery service in 2 hours and the next day TikiNOW for the first time in Southeast Asia, with the same commitment to provide genuine products with a 111% refund policy if counterfeit goods are detected. Established in March 2010, Tiki.vn is currently the top 2 e-commerce site in Vietnam and the top 6 in Southeast Asia. Tiki was in the Top 1 best place to work in Vietnam in the Internet/E-commerce industry 2018 (Anphabe voted), Top 50 best places to work in Asia 2019 (HR Asia voted).

Questions and Answers

What are the key goals and targets that you have set for your supply chain/logistics staff?

- Fulfillment rate of demand
- Mininal waste

- Cost management
- Competitive delivery rate
- Smooth reverse logistics handling
- Efficiency in collaboration

TNSL sharply focuses on providing solutions for fulfillment and delivery — the two critical pieces inside Tiki end-to-end ecommerce ecosystem. It aims for best-in-class services with efficiency in warehouse processes, supply chain, and cost management. It operates with a belief in growing a sustainable business with strong fundamentals, data-driven advanced optimizations to enable all of those. Insights based on data will support the decision-making process as well as service packages to compete against other logistics service providers. Moreover, data-driven tools and platform will enable Tiki attain better reverse logistics handling and waste management. To come up with sound logistics solutions, teaming up with other business functions as well as business partners are very fundamental as it increases the feasibility of the product/service thus resulting in a higher customer satisfaction.

What are the essential skills and competencies for staff in meeting the goals and targets?

- Data analysis
- Customer-oriented and have a high bar of quality
- Information Technology and Automation
- Pressure management
- Teamwork competency

Staffs in this field are working in a heavy data-connected world thus highly analytical and structured thinking is indispensable. This skill is fundamental to evaluate any alternatives for growth or generally to improve any decision-making. In addition, staffs are required to work across functions and be proactive in getting things done. Moreover, jointly work with operational partners to gain knowledge of their circumstances, understand their challenges to find out optimization chances, finalize the problem statement with clear expectations and success measurers, corporate with internal team, such as data analyst to get insights related to challenges; data scientist to research and find potential solutions.

Do you still see these skills are still the same for the next five years? Why or why not? Please elaborate.

Still relevant and more emphasis on:

- Flexibility: embrace and do not resist to change
- Adaptability
- Information Technology Knowledge & Automation

Since July/2021, TNSL has deployed "collaborative robot" application in its operation center with an aim to become the most reliable transportation unit for customers. Robots at TNSL logistics do not replace workers, but on the contrary, robots work, interact, and assist people in difficult tasks. The entire picking process will be automated thanks to the robot. Each robot is responsible for moving smart shelves in a sequence, scientifically and accurately thanks to the barcode system on the floor.

Investing in robots in a challenging period is a strong message from Tiki to affirm the importance of automation in business operation and development, thereby improving service quality to satisfy customer demand. This is an outstanding improvement step of TikiNOW Smart Logistics in digital transformation, helping to cut logistics costs, ensure stability, accuracy, reduce operating hours, improve operational quality, and complete errors. Shortcomings may occur due to human factors, contributing to improving competitiveness. Not only that, TikiNOW Smart Logistics also brings a modern environment, optimizing performance for employees. With that reasons, in the long term, not only people at Tiki but other enterprises in the field have to be ready to learn new things and unlock their potentials with technology advancement. The spirit of "pioneer" is very crucial to find new ways of doing things: more productively and cost-effective. Since connected data, autonomous decisions, and IoT are the essentials of smart logistics, possessing information technology knowledge, and automation still remains critical.

Is there any special skills or competency that supply chain professionals should develop during the pandemic? Please elaborate.

- Information technology knowledge
- Decision-making skills
- Comprehension of market dynamics
- Seeking for continuous improvement

As soon as the Vietnam's economy reopened after the peak of the fourth outbreak of the Coronavirus, a series of new changes occurred in the e-commerce market, with big names having just announced their withdrawal, but also many businesses can mobilize new capital to increase investment, including Tiki.

"86% of users increased their online shopping during and after the quarantine period because of the epidemic. Therefore, investing in such a robot system not only helps us improve the entire e-commerce supply chain, In the long run, we hope to keep costs down." TikiNOW Smart Logistics is one of the pioneers in the race to automate and put robots into logistics operations in Vietnam. With the persistent spirit of the team, Tiki is still striving toward fully automating the most modern warehouse management operation line through technology development and support. If e-commerce is the future industry, then e-logistics is no different from the "backbone" for this industry. With many challenges and difficulties lying ahead, we call for supply chain professionals with agile mindset. In a fast-changing and highly competitive environment with other three leading players in the Vietnamese market who are funded by foreign enterprises like Alibaba and SEA Group, comprehension of market dynamics to exploit new opportunities, coping with the "new normal" and seeking for continous improvement in operation to enrich value propositions especially lock-in Tiki's unique selling point. In fact, Tiki e-commerce platform and Tiki Smart Logistics Company bring a 4.0 sales solution with "Tiki warehouse model — Fulfillment by Tiki (FBT)." Inventory will be activated with TikiNow fast delivery service to ensure delivery time, save warehousing, and order processing costs. The seller only needs to store the goods in the FBT warehouse, the rest of the steps will be responsible by Tiki until the order reaches the buyer. Thanks to this new warehouse model, businesses can save time and manpower, focus on improving service quality, and taking care of products. At the same time, sellers also do not have to worry about operating indicators during operation. For new sellers on the platform, the FBT model will be the ideal choice in terms of cost and profit, ensuring quality service for users. Sellers only need to focus on promoting sales instead of worrying about other issues such as inventory management, order processing, shipping process. Information technology knowledge is indeed truly critical as smart logistics is based on IoTs technology. Moreover, investment in technology will be a solution to many strategic issues related to digitization and digital transformation especially since the outbreak of the global pandemic and other emergency problems. Decision-making thus becomes a key skill here.

Conclusion

In October 2018, Tiki was ranked the second position nationwide in terms of average website visits. According to 2018 statistics, the number of people participating in online shopping in 2018 was 39.9 million people, Vietnam's retail e-commerce revenue reached 8.06 billion USD with a growth rate of up to 30%, a growth largest in the last 3 years.

With a sales policy in line with Vietnamese shopping psychology, Tiki has created trust for customers and is one of the top choices of customers when shopping online. Some impressive numbers that Tiki has achieved are that 85% of customers are satisfied with Tiki's quality and service. This is one of the important factors determining the success of Tiki.

Return policy according to regulations, creating favorable conditions for buyers. With 400,000 customers buying products at Tiki every month, the exchange rate is only 0.95%. Tiki guarantees that the products sold at Tiki are new and 100% genuine. In the rare case that the product customers receive is defective, damaged, or not as described, Tiki is committed to protecting customers with a return and warranty policy.

Established in 2010, after more than 11 years of establishment and development, Tiki has grown to become the leading commercial platform in Vietnam with a scale of nearly 4,000 employees and 20 million registered customers. In November 2021, Tiki successfully "closed an application" for $258 million to invest in Vietnam in the fifth round of capital raising, committing to fully invest in the Vietnamese market, aiming to expand the digital economy, create more jobs, aiming to serve all the needs of Vietnamese people through strengthening the supply chain and developing "Make in Vietnam" technology.

With the current milestones and potential future ahead, especially with e-logistics, people at Tiki, regardless of management level, are encouraged to demonstrate traits of a tranformation future leader who possesses professional, interpersonal, and conceptual skills.

Overall Findings from the Interviews

Logistics industry is a very cost-sensitive and customer-oriented industry. It tries to keep its costs low while meeting customer expectation. From Table 2, we can see the need to auto educe costs. During the pandemic, more workers are advised to work from home but the warehouse operations need people to move cargoes. Thus, the logical option is to explore automation in the warehousing together with

Table 2: Interviewee responses from the logistics industry

Company	A.P. Moller	Siam Cement Logistics	Sitics Logistics Solution	Logistics Company 1	Logistics Company 2	Logistics Company 3	SNT Global logistics	PKT Logistics Group
Country	Vietnam	Thailand	Malaysia	Dubai, UAE	Dubai, UAE	Dubai, UAE	Singapore	Malaysia
Sector	Logistics	Logistics	Logistics	Logistics	Logistics	Logistics	Logistics	Logistics
Position	Logistics Manager	Supply Chain Manager	Director	CEO	General Management	CEO	Director	Director
Key Skills	Data analysis	Soft skills	Systems thinking	Data analysis	Business acumen	Leadership	Scenario planning	Problem solving
Key Skills	Technology automation	Technology automation	Teamwork	Technology automation	Data analysis	Relationship management	Soft skills	Decision-making
Key Skills	Soft skills	Teamwork	Soft skills	Decision-making	Technology automation	Technology automation	Technology automation	Technology automation
Future Skills	Problem solving	Scenario planning	Customer-oriented	Technology automation	Problem solving	Problem solving	Customer-oriented	Systems thinking
Future Skills	Project management	Risk management	Risk management	Change management	Planning	Soft skills	Data analysis	Project management
Future Skills	Customer-oriented	Data analysis	Problem solving	Customer-oriented	Customer-oriented	Process improvement	Decision-making	AI and machine learning
Skills for Pandemic	Crisis management and innovation	Innovation and more visibility	Innovative	E-commerce and agility	E-commerce and technology innovation	Pre-planning and forecasting	Resilent building and collaboration	Proactive and innovative

warehouse management system. With automation, there will be more data available for analysis to optimize its operations. Data analysis becomes another critical skill for this industry to identify performance gaps and improvement. Soft skills are also important to deal with clients as well as motivating employees. This is a labor-intensive industry and soft skills are needed to handle conflicts and manage expectation with clients.

In addition, problem-solving skills and customer oriented are two other competencies that the industry is expecting from the employees. They are troubleshooting issues every day and the problem-solving skills are essential part of the skills to resolve the issues. Since some of the issues will affect the clients, they also need to build good customer relationship. Thus, they need to be customer-oriented to retain the clients as the switching cost is low for them.

Manufacturing industry is faced with material and labor shortages due to the lockdown to prevent the spread of the virus. Most of the interviewees have indicated data analysis as one of the key skillsets to understand more about their processes and customers as shown in Table 3. Some of the interviewees have indicated the need to use the data for ML and AI application. They will help to identify sales trends

Table 3: Interviewee responses from the manufacturing industry

Company	**P&G**	**Cargill**	**Unilever**	**Sri Trang Gloves**	**European connector**	**GS1**
Country	Vietnam	Vietnam	Thailand	Thailand	India	Malaysia
Sector	Manufacturer	Manufacturer	Manufacturer	Manufacturer	Manufacturer	Standards
Position	Supply Chain Manager	Supply Chain Manager	Supply Chain Director	Purchasing Managers	Senior Manager	CEO
Key Skills	Data analysis	Data analysis	Leadership skills	Soft skills	Inventory management	Leadership
Key Skills	Problem solving	Critical thinking	Risk management	Scenario planning	Forecasting	Conflict management
Key Skills	Soft skills	Software application	Data analysis	Data analysis	Software application	Soft skills
Future Skills	Project management	Technology automation	Technology automation	Risk management	Technology automation	Technology automation
Future Skills	Problem solving	Blockchain	Collaboration	Collaboration		Data analysis
Future Skills	Communication skills	Big Data	Scenario planning	Leadership skills		Business acumen
Skills for Pandemic	Crisis management and teamwork	Scenario planning and risk management	Analytical skills	IT skills		Innovation and IT skills

Table 4: Interviewee responses from the trading and retailing industries

Company	Future Group	Zimmer	Central Retail	Giant Distribution	Zespri	Green Renewable
Country	India	India	Vietnam	Malaysia	Singapore	Malaysia
Sector	Retailer	Trading	Trading	Retailer	Agriculture	Agriculture
Position	Senior Manager	Project Manager	Project Manager	Department Head	Supply Chain Director	CEO
Key Skills	Inventory management	Product knowledge	Analytical skill	Inventory management	Process improvement	Project management
Key Skills	Forecasting	Inventory management	Software application	Planning	Collaboration	Planning
Key Skills	Software application	Software application	Relationship management	Software application	Software application	Inventory management
Future Skills	Technology automation	S&OP	Scenario planning	Technology automation	Technology automation	Teamwork
Future Skills	Change management	Financial planning	Data analysis	Data analysis	Performance-driven	Technology automation
Future Skills	Decision-making	Data analysis	Soft skills	Decision-making	Decision-making	Sustainable sourcing
Skills for Pandemic			Problem solving and analytical skills	Resilent building and IT skills	Resilent building and innovative	IT skills

and automate simple decision makings to improve productivity. Many companies are using the data from their ERP system to analyze consumer behavior and automate their processes in line with Industrial 4.0. Soft skills are also important to manage client expectation and collaboration. It is becoming critical to collaborate and jointly forecast with customers and suppliers during this pandemic period where the demand is uncertain. This will ensure a reliable supply chain while attaining a reasonable pricing. The increase in ocean freight rate is an example where some of the supply chain partners are taking advantage of the containers shortage to increase their prices.

Trading and retailing industries are impacted by the disruption in the supply chain. Many of the trader and retailers are running short of inventory due to late delivery. Thus, most of the interviewees are indicating the need to have proper inventory management during this period as shown in Table 4. The need to constantly review and adjust their inventory policies and model is critical for survival as indicated by the interviewees. Most of these companies are using inventory

Table 5: Interviewee responses from e-commerce companies

Company	Chilli Beli	Tiki
Country	Indonesia	Vietnam
Sector	E-commerce	E-commerce
Position	Vice President	Director
Key Skills	System thinking	Data analysis
Key Skills	Soft skills	Documentation
Key Skills	Data Analysis	Software application
Future Skills	Business acumen	Technology automation
Future Skills	Teamwork	Change management
Future Skills	Technology automation	Business acumen
Skills for Pandemic	Explore redundancy and resourceful	Decision-making and IT skills

systems to monitor and plan their inventory. With thousands of SKU to monitor, it makes sense to implement inventory system to manage their inventory and establish policies within the system to optimize the inventory level. Most of the ERP systems today are able to perform complex inventory planning and execution.

For future skills, some of the interviewees believe the data stored in the ERP are currently under-utilized and they can use data analytic for more accurate forecasting and better decision-making. Sales history and costs data are examples of data that can be analyzed for these purposes. In fact, more advance data analytics and visualization are now being deployed to allow supply chain managers to make better decision on utilizing their resources and inventory.

Even though we have managed to interviewed two start-up e-commerce companies, they have similar responses in terms of key skills for this industry. Data analysis is a very critical skills for these companies to learn more about buying behavior. Understanding the strategy to acquire and retain online customers is critical and data can help to explain what strategy works for them. Track and trace are another essential feature for e-commerce companies and the data collected can be used to determine the bottlenecks. Another important skill is to understand the business model and adjust the model to compete effectively online. Some of the e-commerce companies are building redundancy during this period to avoid inventory shortages while others are decentralizing their warehouses in case of lockdown.

Additional Interviews

We have conducted additional interviews with companies based in China (software provider), Brunei (food and beverage chain), Bangladesh (maritime operator) and Pakistan (aviation operator), and compiled the results in Appendix D.

Discussion

The analysis of data and the ability to implement advanced technologies are essential skills indicated by all the interviewees. The ability to keep supply chains optimized and future-ready is essential to uninterrupted functioning and expansion of businesses worldwide. Nothing has helped supply chains leap ahead in this endeavor like data has. Smart sensors, AI, and various business intelligence (BI) tools help ensure supply visibility, shipping at low costs, forecast demand, and control inventory. Business intelligence and data analytics, when used strategically, can enable cost reduction and boost efficiency across business functions. Supply chain, for instance, is one such function that can benefit enormously with the use of data analytics. The biggest benefit of real-time data and analytics lies in the fact that it can help you understand your supply chain inside out. In turn, this can help you make informed and strategic decisions in times of uncertainty.

Here are a few key supply chain metrics that can be discovered by using data analytics:

Examples of supply-side metrics and insights

- Your suppliers' production capacities
- Cost variations for different levels of capacity
- The reliability and resilience of your supplier's suppliers (especially during crises)
- Alternative sources of supply
- Your inventory management capabilities
- Degree of traceability across your entire supply chain

Examples of demand-side metrics and insights

- The customer's purchasing power
- Competitor pricing of the same service or product line
- Consumer behavior, preferences, and usage trends
- Customer relationships that need attention
- Accurate demand forecasting and inventory distribution

Think of the derived benefits — reduced communication gaps between suppliers and manufacturers, faster deliveries, improved service levels, and reduced costs. It is no wonder many enterprises are tapping into the value data analytics has to offer.

Chapter 3

Supply Chain Skills and Competency from the Online Job Advertisements

Introduction

Technical diffusion, globalization, and the internet revolution have all increased the expansion of online transactions and changed business operation systems in recent years. The Internet and the rise of computer technology have altered the way firms operate. One area that has been substantially affected by information technology as a result of the phenomenon is online job posting advertisement, often known as e-recruiting. Furthermore, as a result of the current COVID-19 outbreak, a new necessity for a long-term contactless replacement in business operation systems has evolved. Through an online job posting advertisement, this chapter gives an exploratory assessment into the employability skills set requirement. The goal of this chapter is to identify and categories any commonalities in the requirements for employability skills in the logistics and supply chain industry. This is accomplished by analyzing the content of online job advertising advertisements. The top 10 skills required by employers for logistics and supply chain positions in this study are supply chain analytical, technological aptitude, teamwork skills, customer focus, leadership skills, interpersonal skills, people skills, creativity and resilience, demand and supply forecasting and project management skills as well as soft skills and hard skills which are both preferred by employers.

Overview of Skills and Competency from the Online Job Advertisements

The development of the COVID-19 epidemic, as well as the implementation of measures like lockdown and working from home, has boosted internet usage and changed business operations systems (Nayal *et al.*, 2021). As a result, the internet's user base has exploded since its commercial launch in 1991. The Internet has altered the way businesses operate, especially how they find and hire personnel. The use of internet platforms for job posting and advertisement transactions has increased dramatically during the last decade. By boosting job seekers' access to the required set of employability abilities, information technology, and internet platforms have increased impulse job-seeking activity. Due to that, job posting advertisement, also known as e-recruiting, has grown in importance as a major Internet business tool. This is due in part to the ease of access, increased efficiency, lower costs, and chances for job searchers (Rodrigues and Martinez, 2020).

The practice of recruiting using commercial job sites or firm websites that promotes employment possibilities, set requirements for employable abilities, and retrieve possible employee information is known as online job posting advertisement (Tan and Laswad, 2018). Posting positions, accepting resumes, administering screening tests, and communicating with prospective applicants are all done online. Unlike conventional methods, the Internet is now a prominent technique of recruiting potential employees, with online competition for qualified people. This may not sound weird, but LinkedIn, the most popular professional social networking site, today has about 740 million members in 200 countries, with over 55 million firms registered (Davis *et al.*, 2020). The increased use of internet job posting advertisements as a commercial tool has influenced both parties involved, especially during the COVID-19 pandemic.

Online job posting advertising may be defined as a critical function of human resource management that is used to find the best people and encourage job seekers to apply for open positions in the company. It is the process of determining the required set of employable abilities, obtaining an acceptable number of employees, and making an effective selection among the applicants. A social networking site is a website that allows users to share and collaborate on digital content in virtual communities. LinkedIn, Facebook, Instagram, Pinterest, Snapchat, Twitter, and a few others are some of the most popular social networking sites for online job searching (de Gottal and Bonny, 2019). Social media job posting advertisement is not only beneficial to the company, but it may also be beneficial to job seekers.

The requirements for employability skills in the twenty-first-century business world are more complex and varied than in the past. The world has become a seamless global market environment because of advancements in information and communication technologies. In order to meet global market needs, skill development has become a critical component of employability. Any applicant will be shaped into a person with employable qualities through a well-balanced combination of hard skills and soft skills to achieve greater success at work (Ibrahim *et al.*, 2017). Personal characteristics, adaptability, emotional intelligence, core knowledge skills, technological advancement skill, and a few other factors are all considered in a holistic view of employability skills. Employability skills have been a focal point among employers as a result of the information economy, globalization, and changing job market conditions. This chapter deals with the study of current career opportunities in the logistics and supply chain industry and investigates the most employable skill set required in the logistics and supply chain industry via online job posting advertisements.

In this investigation, data were collected from 2021 for job postings in Malaysia and Indonesia. The following sources were used to identify comparable online job posting advertisements: (i) LinkedIn, (ii) Indeed, and (iii) Robert Walters in the logistics and supply chain-related industries. The main reason authors focus on these three main portals is due to its examined the job advertisements on the managerial positions. The study calculated the number of job openings in the field. Content analysis was performed to analyze the employability skills set requirement through online job posting advertisements to achieve the second research objective. Several phases were involved in the screening process namely including and excluding job posting advertisements from various databases, as well as removing duplicate job posting advertisements (similar job posting advertisements found in different databases).

Job Postings for Logistics and Supply Chain Professionals in Malaysia

The first round of screening yielded a total of 246 job advertising advertisements. A total of 52 job posting advertisements were rejected because the selection criteria were not met; 194 job posting advertisements were eligible for the screening process.

During the collection period, the study discovered that 187 managerial-related positions were advertised on LinkedIn, 31 jobs were advertised on Indeed, and 28 jobs were advertised in Robert Walters. Supply chain manager roles were the most sought after, with a total of 42 opportunities available throughout all Malaysian states. It is followed by Warehouse Manager posts, which have 39 openings, and Production Planning Manager posts, which have 26 openings. Based on the survey, job possibilities are concentrated in Kuala Lumpur, Selangor, and Penang, which account for over 84% of all job openings in Malaysia. It is followed by Johor Bahru, which accounted for nearly 10% of all job opportunities. The majority of business activity in Malaysia is centered in a few major cities such as Kuala Lumpur, Selangor, Penang, and Johor Bahru; therefore, these findings are not surprising. The results of the job opportunity major cities availability survey are displayed in Figure 2.

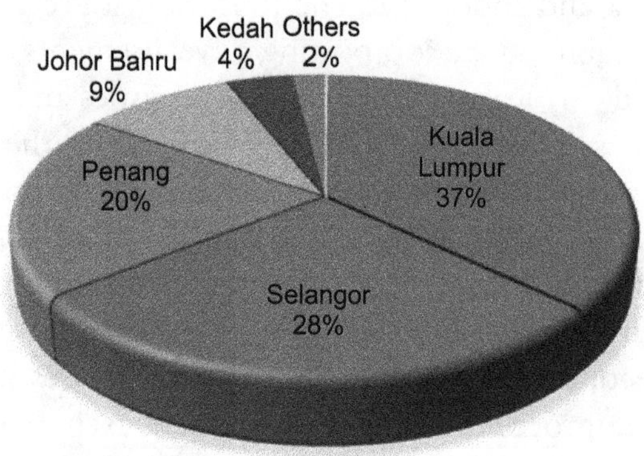

Figure 2: Major cities for logistics and supply chain industry job opportunities

Except for the four major cities stated previously, the results in Figure 2 show that job opportunities are limited in other states. The findings of this study are in line with Siwar *et al.* (2016), who found that urban development in Malaysia has been concentrated in a few large metropolitan centers. Furthermore, the Malaysian government has liberalized its trade policies in recent decades in response to intense pressure from global market economies. The initiative allows corporations to concentrate their operations in and around a few major Malaysian cities such as Kuala Lumpur, Selangor, Penang, and Johor Bahru. Where development is restricted, there will be fewer firms and, as a result, fewer job opportunities. Meanwhile, Table 6 summarizes the advertised logistics and supply chain-related job titles.

Employability, according to Pham (2021), is a set of abilities, understandings, personal characteristics, and the ability to operate well in one's chosen employment, which helps the individual, the workforce, the community, and the economy. This section reveals the findings on the category of employability abilities that firms in the logistics and supply chain industry require of potential workers. A total of 187 job posting advertisements were gathered from LinkedIn, Indeed, and Robert Walters Malaysia, and the results were compiled. The information on a list of employability skills was gathered from the suitable advertisements as listed in Table 7. The number of times each employability skill was discovered in the advertisements was quantified using a quantitative count.

A total of 20 primary employability skills were identified from the content analysis of the logistics and supply chain job posting advertisement. According to the findings, the top five most in-demand employable skills in logistics and supply chain are (i) supply chain analytical, (ii) technological aptitude, (iii) teamwork skills, (iv) customer focus, and (v) leadership skills. The top five skills identified in the study are very important for logistics and supply chain professionals. In the current circumstances, logistics and supply chain professionals, for example, should guarantee those firm objectives are achieved and the revenue is optimized in order to remain competitive. Firms can utilize supply chain analytics to solve a variety of supply chain issues. Some of the supply chain analytical examples include capacity planning, advanced sales and operations planning, demand shaping, and a few others.

Table 6: Job opportunities (managerial level) in logistics and supply chain industry

Job Title	Job Opportunities
Supply chain	42
Warehouse management	39
Production planning	26
Transportation	12
Inventory/materials management	7
Information technology/system advanced user	6
Sourcing/procurement management	6
Retail logistics	5
Product innovation	5
Project management	5
E-commerce	5
Category management	4
Trade compliance/governance	4
Analyst demand planning	4
Operations management	4
Customer experience	4
Shipping	4
Process improvement or business excellence	3
Manufacturing technical	3
Environmental health safety	2
ERP specialist	2
Import/export	2
Total	194

Furthermore, in today's logistics and supply chain industry, technological aptitude is frequently exploited. To carry out the day-to-day operations, logistics and supply chain professionals must be technologically sophisticated. Blockchain, the IoT, artificial intelligence (AI), and machine learning are examples of technology that are extensively employed in the industry. While performing their jobs, logistics and

Table 7: Top 20 logistics and supply chain industry employability skills requirement

Item	Skills
1.	Supply chain analytical
2.	Technological aptitude
3.	Teamwork skills
4.	Customer focus
5.	Leadership skills
6.	Interpersonal skills
7.	People skills
8.	Creativity and resilience
9.	Demand and supply forecasting
10.	Project management
11.	Transportation/fleet management
12.	Warehouse management
13.	Asset and inventory management
14.	Reverse logistics
15.	Negotiation skills
16.	Communication skills
17.	Emotional intelligence
18.	Adaptability skills
19.	Time management
20.	Knowledge of new social and digital media

supply chain professionals should arm themselves with some knowledge of technology as designed by the designers. Teamwork skills, customer focus, and leadership abilities, on the other hand, are critical for logistics and supply chain professionals because such skills assist them to efficiently coordinate and improve their day-to-day business operations. Practitioners in the field of logistics and SCM must connect and collaborate with their teams from diverse corporate departments. It is critical to ensure that projects are managed properly and efficiently in order to respond more quickly to the changes in market demand and supply chain conditions. As a result, teamwork skills are a must-have for each professional.

Furthermore, in logistics, good customer service is dependent on clear communication as well as on timely and damage-free deliveries. Customer service in the logistics and supply chain is critical to the smooth operation of the overall business. Hence, customer focus is essential to the success of the business. Moreover, leadership skills are important to promote, encourage, and incentivize innovation and initiative among the employees and partners throughout the supply chain operations. Ideally, leadership skills are critical for promoting, encouraging, and incentivizing creativity and initiative among employees and partners across the supply chain. Good communication skills, change management skills, and the ability to inspire cooperation are ideal leadership skills that allow for the creation of an atmosphere that fosters creativity and cross-departmental collaboration that benefits all parties involved.

Job Postings for Logistics and Supply Chain Professionals in Indonesia

The sample size for this research is 60 job advertisements, with 38 job advertisements from the logistics users, 12 job advertisements from companies in the logistics providers, 10 job advertisements from companies in the service industry, and 10 job advertisements from companies in the service or consulting industry. We are not only looking at the job requirements area of the job adverts but also the section where the companies explain what the supply chain managers would be doing in the organization. In order to obtain a job, supply chain managers must prepare for a key component of the job search and this is a job qualification that assesses the capabilities of supply chain manager applicants.

Following an evaluation of the 56 separate skill sets and qualifications, it was determined that some of the same skill sets and job qualifications were required in a number of different job advertisements, showing that there are 56 distinct skill sets and qualifications in job advertisements. Using Microsoft Excel, the data were analyzed using a spreadsheet that was created to correspond with the job advertisements

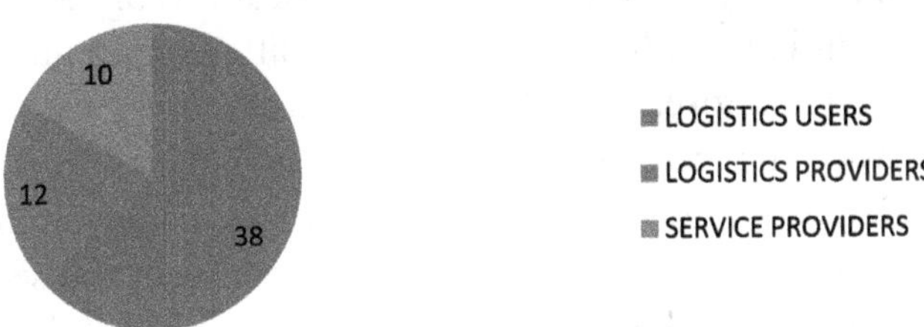

Figure 3: Respondents by industry

that had been compiled. The spreadsheet included some job qualifications and skill sets that were created to match the job advertisements that had been compiled. We make use of a spreadsheet in order to map and match skill sets and job qualifications with enterprises and organizations. The skills and job credentials are listed in the rows of the spreadsheet, and the names of the various companies are included in the columns.

When 60 job advertisements were subjected to a thorough data analysis, it was determined that there are certain skill sets that the majority of employers are seeking, with more than 20 job adverts specifically specifying these specific skill sets. Oral communication (32 job advertisements), transportation/fleet management, and people skills (24 job advertisements), supply chain analytics (21 job advertisements), and fluency in other languages (English and Chinese) are among the skill

Table 8: Critical skills for supply chain professionals in the manufacturing industry

Skills	Job Postings
Oral communication	22
Leadership skills	15
Transportation/fleet management	15
Fluency in other languages (English or Chinese)	15
Asset and inventory management	14

sets required (20 job advertisements). In contrast, the data that were analyzed did not fully represent the job qualifications of each organization, because different industries may require different job qualifications and skill sets. Therefore, the information gathered will be profiled in accordance with the categories into which it is classified. It is classified as follows: data from firms that are logistics users, data from firms that are logistics suppliers, and data from organizations in the service and consulting industries. The data categories are then subdivided into multinational corporations (MNCs) and local enterprises in order to calculate the job qualifications for each industry and category.

Organizations that rely on 3PL services, as well as companies who provide some logistical services directly to their clients up to a certain level, fall under this particular category. Organizations in the industrial and e-commerce industries, among other industries, are among those who use logistics services. Indeed, 38 job vacancies in the logistics business have been posted by organizations in the industry. The data mapping that was accomplished in the spreadsheet led to the identification of some job requirements that some companies are seeking for. Examples include companies that are searching for individuals who can manage fleets and carry materials for their logistical operations, among other things. It is vital for SCM applicants to have prior experience in this skill set in order to ensure that their things are delivered to customers on time. Because fleet management is related with cost-effectiveness and efficiency, it is a good investment. Other key aspects include the scheduling and tracking of the products that are delivered to customers, and successful fleet management can contribute to an improvement in customer satisfaction. As indicated by the 22 job advertisements, applicants for supply chain manager positions should have strong communication skills, particularly oral communication skills, among other qualifications. Because supply chain managers are regularly obliged to communicate with their subordinates as well as 3PL suppliers, this is a common misunderstanding (3PL providers). For manufacturing and e-commerce businesses, verbal communication skills are essential, and oral communication skills are essential for logistics companies as well. This is because logistics companies typically require managers to be able to communicate effectively with their subordinates and coordinate with them effectively in order to achieve the company's goals. Leadership ability, in addition to oral communication skills, is critical in ensuring that information sharing can take place in a healthy manner and that employees can exchange knowledge at the appropriate level. Good oral communication skills mixed with strong leadership abilities can ensure that a company has a strong team and that a department is well-managed. Because of this, there are 15 job postings that declare as a criterion that candidates for supply chain manager positions possess this particular skill set.

The other job requirement that distinguishes enterprises in the logistics users' group is that the vast majority of companies demand supply chain managers to manage the company's inventory, with 14 job advertisements asking this skill set in total. Because logistics users often monitor product inventories, candidates for SCM positions should be able to do so. And most companies in this category are manufacturing companies, which they need the supply chain managers to ensure the availability of the inventory, so that they can manufacture their products. Inventory management is constantly concerned with optimizing the inventory in order to produce good firm performance, boost effectiveness, and efficiency, among other goals. Furthermore, inadequate inventory management on the manufacturing floor may result in excess or shortages of raw materials, which will have an indirect impact on the company's overall performance.

There are some employment criteria that are not specified in the job postings, such as change management, ISO 14000 standards, reverse logistics, quantitative modeling skills, and circular economy. As for ISO, most organizations would want someone to be in charge of the application of the ISO standards, which would not be included in the job description of supply chain managers in the first place and the application of ISO 14000 is still limited in Indonesia, primarily because it is a rule that cannot be regulated due to the large number of firms with varying levels of quality that need to be standardized in Indonesia. As a part of the supply chain's spectrum, reverse logistics is required to be there; nevertheless, it is not yet a significant issue that supply chain managers in Indonesia should be aware of according to the Environmental Impact Agency (BAPEDAL). In Indonesia, supply

Table 9: Critical skills for supply chain professionals in the logistics industry

Skills	Job Posting
Warehouse management	7
People skills	6
Oral communication	6
Relationship management	5
Transportation/fleet management	5

chain managers are not expected to have quantitative modeling abilities or to be familiar with circular economy principles because most companies delegate this responsibility to the finance department. There is also no job advertisements stating that they need e-procurement skill possessed by the supply chain manager applicants.

3PL organizations and shipping corporations predominate in the Logistics Providers category, which covers companies in the transportation and logistics sector. Because they typically provide logistical services for other businesses that wish to ship their products but do not have the resources to do so, even though the sample taken is small, the companies that posted the job postings represent the Indonesian logistics provider industry, according to the findings. Whereas companies in the logistics users category are looking for supply chain managers who will be able to collaborate with 3PL providers to plan and optimize a distribution route and schedule, companies in the logistics providers category are looking for supply chain managers whose primary responsibilities will be communication skills as well as warehouse and fleet management. Due to the importance of warehouse management for logistics providers, there are seven job postings looking for supply chain managers who are competent of managing a warehouse on Indeed.com. As a result of the fact that logistics providers are storing the products that they want to deliver in a warehouse, and because the efficiency of the delivery process is greatly enhanced by having a properly managed warehouse, having a properly managed warehouse can make the product delivery process run more efficiently. Logistics firms typically have many warehouses to oversee in order to better serve their customers, and this can make the product delivery process run more efficiently. A number of job ads specify that applicants must have experience in fleet management and transportation. This is proven by the fact that these skills are required for applicants in five job postings. In order to ensure customer satisfaction, supply chain managers are responsible for the planning and scheduling of transportation and delivery fleets. As a result, they must ensure that products are delivered as efficiently as possible. It almost always has something to do with the route and truckloads; effectively planning and scheduling truckloads can result in cost reduction and time savings throughout the transportation process.

These results are consistent with the findings of a previous study conducted by Murphy and Poist (1991a), who discovered that logistics skill sets are required for supply chain manager applicants in order to be considered qualified. Warehouse management, fleet management, and fleet or transportation management are some of the logistics skill sets that are required. A strong interpersonal competence, such as people skills, is expected of supply chain managers who work in logistics companies. In fact, there are six job ads specifically requesting that applicants possess this skill set in order to be considered. According to Giunipero and Pearcy (2000), people skills are essential for firms in order for supply chain managers to effectively coordinate with their subordinates and employees. Because of the nature of the company, which necessitates a considerable amount of labor to deliver the items, the logistics staffs are regarded as the first line of defense in the operations of the logistics companies they support. Additionally, there are six companies looking for supply chain managers that are strong communicators, particularly in oral communication. Additionally, five job postings requested that applicants for supply chain manager positions possess strong written communication skills. These findings align with previous researches (Gibson *et al.*, 1998), which stated that communication and interpersonal skill are one of the important skill sets for the supply chain managers in logistics industry.

The consulting industry dominates the service provider category, with the consulting business accounting for the vast majority of companies in the category. In order to discover people who can work as

Table 10: Critical skills for supply chain professionals in service providers

Skills	Job Posting
Supply chain analytics	7
People skills	5
Production planning and scheduling	5
Supply chain process reengineering/optimization	5

consultants in service provider businesses, service providers often post job adverts on job boards. The job posts presented as samples in this area come from significant organizations that represent the service provider industry, which is another plus. Taking this as an example, service provider businesses are searching for supply chain managers that can assist them in advising and assisting their clients by providing advice and solutions. Supply chain analytics is one skill set that sticks out in the data analysis that has been completed and it is one that should not be overlooked. Approximately 7 out of every 10 job postings in the service provider business require this specific skill set to be present. A critical skill set in supply chain analytics is that of data collection and analysis. The information gathered will assist the customer in properly planning their supply chain, and the consulting firms will be able to provide appropriate advice and solutions to their customers in order to assist the clients' businesses in growing. The vast majority of job advertisements placed by service provider companies are for experienced supply chain managers with a minimum of 6–12 years of relevant experience in the relevant industry, according to the most recent data. A different skill set is required of supply chain managers in service provider organizations compared to supply chain managers in other industries. Additionally, service provider companies are looking for applicants who have the ability to optimize or reengineer supply chain processes, who have good people skills, and who have the knowledge to perform planning and scheduling for manufacturing operations, among other qualifications. Each of these skill sets is listed on five different job adverts. When it comes to supply chain optimization, clients of service

Table 11: Critical skills for supply chain professionals in multinational companies

Skills	Job Posting
Oral communication	24
People skills	20
Leadership skills	15
Distribution planning and management	14
Supply Chain Analytics	14

provider organizations are often looking for consultants that can provide them with advice on how to increase the efficacy and efficiency of their supply chain process, according to the industry standard. When it comes to providing expertise to consumers, the consulting sector relies on its understanding of production planning and scheduling. To top it all off, service provider firms are looking for supply chain managers who have great people skills or interpersonal talents in order to communicate and understand the needs of their clients as well as be willing to provide a helping hand when required by the company. Most consulting and service provider businesses look for applicants that have a knowledge-based skill set rather than a technical skill set, according to a recent survey. This is due to the fact that consulting firms are more concerned with offering advice and solutions that are suited to the specific requirements of their clients.

Furthermore, we divide some organizations into several groups based on the extent of their operations, which is explained in detail in the book. It is vital to distinguish between these companies because they may require a variety of work certifications and skill sets depending on the scope of their operations. In total, there are 60 job advertisements collected, with 38 of them coming from global firms (MNCs). Multinational firms are frequently on the lookout for employees with a more advanced skill set and job credentials. In particular, there are 24 job postings from MNCs that are looking for persons with great oral communication skills to serve as supply chain managers in this situation, according to the data. To be successful, management teams in these firms needed to be able to communicate effectively with others, including other departments and, most crucially, with employees and subordinates in order to achieve success. As a result, there are 20 job advertisements for SCM positions that require candidates to have people skills, and 15 job advertisements for supply chain manager positions that require applicants to have leadership abilities. A well-managed supply chain department is essential for a company's success and this requires that the company's supply chain managers possess a set of specific competencies. Twenty job adverts specified that applicants must be able to communicate fluently in a language other than Bahasa, according to the research conducted by Thai *et al.* (2011). Thai *et al.* (2011) did research in a place where English is the native language, which contrasts with their findings, which were conducted in a country where English is not the native language.

For supply chain managers working for multinational organizations, it is essential and desirable that they be able to communicate effectively on a global scale. There are also 14 job openings for supply chain managers who are capable of performing distribution planning and management, which is necessary because most MNCs have a complex supply chain that comprises enterprises in several jurisdictions. Furthermore, supply chain managers are responsible for the planning and management of distribution, as well as the integration of distribution across a number of different countries. A supply chain manager is often sought after by MNCs for the purpose of planning, managing, and integrating the supply chains that these companies maintain. This is due to the fact that supply chain networks are complicated and necessitate the application of specialist knowledge. As a result, supply chain managers are primarily concerned with managerial tasks rather than technical ones, which is understandable. Fourteen job postings specifically request that applicants for supply chain manager positions have the ability to handle fleets or transportation, which is not surprising considering that fleet and transportation management is a logistics skill set that a supply chain manager should possess. There are an additional 14 job postings that specify that applicants must possess supply chain analytics as a skill set. This is due to the fact that multinational businesses (MNCs) are

Table 12: Critical skills for supply chain professionals in local companies

Skills	Job Posting
Transportation/fleet management	10
Oral communication	8
Leadership skills	7
Warehouse management	7
Supply chain analytics	7

increasingly focusing on worldwide expansion, and in order to be successful, managers must be able to examine the supply chain and make informed decisions.

Job advertisements from local Indonesian enterprises with no overseas branches account for the majority of the remaining job advertisements (22 out of 60 total job advertisements collected). In contrast to MNCs, which have a presence in numerous countries, companies in this category are often focused on their local markets and have just a single country of operation. They are searching for supply chain managers who will be able to handle transportation and fleet management as well as the rest of their duties. The skillset in question is being sought after by 10 job postings, each of which requires a distinct set of credentials that varies from those required by multinational organizations. In addition, there are seven employment openings that require someone with warehouse management skills to complement their transportation and fleet management expertise. Neither of these is technical logistics abilities, but they are both necessary for any effective supplier management expert. Following the investigation, local enterprises frequently require higher technical work credentials, and the supply chain managers employed by these organizations are more active in the supply chain processes of their individual companies. because they are more concerned with carrying out their day-to-day operations Moreover, seven other job postings from local businesses seek supply chain managers with excellent leadership talents and the ability to lead a supply chain team, as supply chain managers are responsible for ensuring that the company's entire supply chain process operates smoothly. Because of this, there are seven job postings on Indeed for supply chain managers who possess supply chain analytics expertise. This is due to the fact that many small firms desire to grow their operations while also remaining knowledgeable about the market and the industry as a whole. Oral communication is another key skill set to have for supply chain manager applicants, as evidenced by the fact that eight job posts specifically specified that this particular skill set was required in order to be a supply chain manager in their respective firms. Having high oral communication skills has been demonstrated to be a valuable asset for managers because it allows them to communicate effectively with their subordinates, other departments, and even other parties involved.

Discussion

Analytical skills, technological aptitude, teamwork skills, customer focus, and leadership skills are all common skills sought by businesses in the logistics and supply chain professions based on this study. Soft skills are the most important of these needed skills. This study would be beneficial to job seekers in terms of better equipping themselves with skills that fit the changing needs of contemporary businesses. Employers are looking for well-rounded employees. Employees with superior soft and hard skills have an advantage in the employment market. Nonetheless, this study provides a platform for raising awareness about the importance of online job posting advertisements in providing job seekers with the employability skill set those employers required.

Some skill sets that were most frequently used in the research conducted by Thai *et al.* (2011) are also sought after by some job advertisements in this research, including problem-solving ability and managing customer relationships, according to the findings of this research. However, according to the findings of this study, certain skill sets are not commonly seen in the data collected. Furthermore, this research is consistent with the findings of Gammelgaard and Larson (2001), who stated that oral communication is a skill that should be prioritized in educational settings. In addition, according to their research, there are three skill sets that the majority of firms seek: interpersonal or managerial skills, quantitative or technology abilities, and SCM core competencies. In this particular instance, the research discovered that interpersonal skills and SCM core skills are the most frequently mentioned talents in the job listings that were discovered.

Chapter 4

Supply Chain Skills and Competency from the Online Survey

Introduction

This chapter empirically examines the supply chain present and future skills and competencies expected of supply chain managers in Asia. First, a comprehensive survey instrument comprising of 50 skills and competencies across 10 categories was developed through an extensive literature review. Next, using data collected through an online survey, the relative importance of supply chain managers' present and future skills and competencies was understood. Further, a gap analysis was conducted to identify the present and future skill and competency gaps. Overall, the findings provide a road map for organizations and educators looking to develop the essential skills and competencies of supply chain managers for managing the present and future supply chains. It also enables organizations to make changes in their hiring, training, and retention strategies of supply chain managers. While the study was conducted in Asia, the supply chain skills and competencies listed in this study and their categorization can be employed in different settings.

Overview Skills and Competency from the Online Survey

SCM has emerged as one of the primary factors in determining the competitiveness of organizations. This is because, in today's competitive environment, businesses have realized that the competition is no longer dependent solely on the capabilities of individual companies but on the capability of a tightly integrated supply chain (Prajogo and Sohal, 2013). The role of supply chain managers, therefore, is crucial to businesses. Hence, not surprisingly, supply chain managers' skills and competencies have attracted increasing attention from practitioners and scholars in recent years (Shou and Wang, 2017). This is because demand for supply chain talent is at an all-time high, as more and more companies have recognized how vital SCM is to their success (DHL, 2021). There is no doubt that supply chain managers play a pivotal role in achieving a firm's operational and strategic goals and thereby directly contributing to its financial performance and future competitiveness (Shou and Wang, 2017). Although past studies have examined the supply chain managers skills and competencies (Gammelgaard and Larson, 2001; Mangan and Christopher, 2005; Thai *et al.*, 2012), it is apparent that supply chain managers nowadays are responsible for managing far more complex supply chains with broader coverage and functionalities than in the past (Shou and Wang, 2017). Moreover, the competition and challenges facing modern supply chains are far more severe than before. Therefore, the skills and competencies expected of contemporary supply chain managers are expected to be different than those in the past.

For instance, the ongoing supply chain disruptions due to the COVID-19 pandemic and related restrictions have posed significant challenges for supply chains globally and have threatened the supply of a whole range of goods, from food and beverages to consumer electronics. Companies have been faced with substantial business and operational disruptions, which have included everything from mitigating the effects of reduced supply to managing disruptions to logistics suppliers, and indeed hurdles in meeting their own contractual obligations to customers. It revealed the vulnerabilities of production and supply chain strategies across the world. Bottlenecks were seen in every link of the supply chain. For instance, clogged ports, widespread shortages of shipping containers and warehouse capacity, and a lack of truck drivers to move goods have led to record order backlogs across major supply chain hubs. Still, organizations have relied on their supply chain managers to lead them out of the COVID-19 crisis despite generating new uncertainties. While many supply chain managers successfully navigated the crisis, others were not so successful in managing the crisis, and have faltered under pressure, resulting in temporary or permanent business closures. The heterogeneity in the success of firms during the COVID-19 has reemphasized the importance of having strong supply chain managers during a crisis, which enabled organizations to seize the opportunities presented by the crisis and stay ahead of the competition.

Unfortunately, supply chains around the globe, in almost every region and industry sector, are facing a severe talent shortage that threatens those companies' very livelihoods as the demand for supply chain managers are far exceeding available supply as Baby Boomers retire (Forbes, 2018; DHL, 2021). According to a recent study, organizations are finding it difficult to fill senior-level SCM positions. There are six available jobs for every qualified supply chain manager (DHL, 2021). The shortage of supply chain managers with the requisite broad set of skills to satisfy ongoing demand can be primarily attributed to many firms placing more emphasis on cost reduction and improving relationships with customers and suppliers than on developing people to achieve their supply chain objectives (Ellinger and Ellinger, 2014).

At the same time, the future skills and competencies needed are changing rapidly (Forbes, 2018). This is because supply chains have experienced significant and rapid changes in recent years. These changes are driven by several factors, including business environment, globalization, short product life cycles, increased outsourcing, technological advances, particularly Internet-based systems, increased demands for delivering superior operational performance, and of course, the ongoing COVID-19 pandemic. Yet, most organizations haven't changed their hiring, training, and retention methods. Some of the skills and competencies that are critical to running supply chains in 5 years may be different from today. Still, organizations continue to screen and select supply chain managers by checking off lots of boxes of keywords that correspond with required experiences that likely will have nothing to do with the role in the near future (Forbes, 2018).

Hence, employers will benefit from the knowledge on the critical skills and competencies that supply chain managers must possess for selecting, training, and retaining competent supply chain managers to manage current supply chains and future supply chains. The relevance of employing competent supply chain managers is even greater for firms operating in emerging markets (DHL, 2021). Unfortunately, most previous studies on SCM skills and competencies have focused on developed, western countries such as Australia, United Kingdom, France, and the United States (Gammelgaard and Larson, 2001; Mangan and Christopher, 2005; Prajogo and Sohal, 2013; Tatham *et al.*, 2017). Limited studies that focused on emerging economies in Asia have mainly focused only on one country, such as India (Dubey and Gunasekaran, 2015) or Singapore (Thai *et al.*, 2012). Empirical investigation covering multiple countries appears to be limited in the literature, thereby limiting the generalizability of the study findings. This study aims to fill the gap in the literature by conducting a comprehensive, multicountry investigation on the present and future skills and competencies of supply chain managers in Asia and seek to bridge the gap between present and future skills and competencies for supply chain managers. The specific research questions of this study are as follows:

1. What skills and competencies are expected of supply chain managers to manage present supply chains effectively?
2. What skills and competencies are expected of supply chain managers to manage future supply chains effectively?
3. The extent of the present and future skills and competencies gap among supply chain managers?

A survey-based research approach was adopted in this study to assess the present and future (in the next 5 years) skills and competencies expected of supply chain managers. This method facilitated structured data collection from a large representative sample population, which is critical for enhancing the generalizability of the findings (Al Ahbabi *et al.*, 2019). The survey had three sections. The first section captured the demographic profile of the respondents and their organization. The second section captured the respondent's perceptions of present supply chain skills and competencies, while the third section captured the respondent's perceptions of future supply chain skills expected of supply chain managers. For sections 2 and 3 in the survey, the 50 underlying items identified in the literature across the 10 categories are used. A 5-point Likert-type scale, ranging from 1 — not all important;

2 — slightly important; 3 — moderately important; 4 — very important, and 5 — extremely important, was employed to capture respondent's perceptions. A sample question to capture the present skills and competencies is "Please rate the importance of 'demand forecasting' for you as a supply chain manager to remain competitive in the current scenario." Similarly, a sample question to capture the future skills and competencies is "Please rate the importance of 'demand forecasting' for you as a supply chain manager to remain competitive in the next five years."

During the development phase of the survey instrument, the questionnaire was pretested with one industry leader (Head of Supply Chain) and two academic experts with knowledge in this domain. The pretest process with the participants involved checking the appropriateness of the questions, survey flow, evaluating the readability/choice of terminology, clarity, and ease of understanding on the intended objective of the question, and the practical relevance of the items in real-world situations (Balasubramanian and Shukla, 2017). Feedback and suggestions from the pretest respondents were helpful in validating and improving the survey instrument.

The main survey was administrated via Qualtrics, an online survey system, for a period of two months, from September 2021 to October 2021. In terms of sampling, both convenient sampling and snowball nonprobability sampling techniques were used to recruit global participants via email and social media platforms. A total of 265 participants from 22 countries (where they live and work) responded to the survey. Since the study focuses on supply chain managers in Asia, we excluded respondents from non-Asia countries such as France, the United States, and the United Kingdom, leaving 187 responses. To ensure quality responses, we excluded participants who responded (less than 10 years of experience) to the question — "How many years of experience do you have as a supply chain/logistics professional?" leaving 120 usable responses from 12 Asian countries for our data analyses. Although there are no strict guidelines on the sample size for statistical analysis, a sample size of 100–150 with no missing values was found to provide valid results with reasonable generalizability (Anderson and Gerbing, 1988). The demographic details of the survey respondents are given in Table 13.

Table 13: Demographic classification of survey respondents

Personal Details	Responses	Percentage
Gender		
Male	82	68.3
Female	38	31.7
Age		
25–34	42	35.0
35–44	34	28.3
45–54	28	23.3
55 and above	16	13.3
Education		
High school/diploma	8	6.7
Bachelor's degree	38	31.7
Master's degree	70	58.3
PhD/doctoral degree	4	3.3
Position/level in organization		
Mid level	36	30.0
Senior level	47	39.2
Top management/leadership	37	30.8
Experience in the current organization		
0–12 months	29	24.2
1–3 years	28	23.3
4–5 years	21	17.5
6–10 years	14	11.7
Greater than 10 years	28	23.3
Firm details		
Number of employees		
Less than 100	31	25.8
100–249	15	12.5
250–499	12	10.0
500–999	12	10.0
1000 or more	50	41.7

Table 13: (*Continued*)

Personal Details	Responses	Percentage
Firm type		
Private sector firm (local/home-grown)	36	30.0
Private sector firm (subsidiary of a foreign/multinational firm)	53	44.2
Private sector firm (joint venture between foreign and local firm)	12	10.0
Public sector firm	9	7.5
Semi-government firm	5	4.2
Others	5	4.2
Industry sector		
Transportation and logistics	46	38.3
Manufacturing	26	21.7
Information technology	9	7.5
Retail and trading	7	5.8
Healthcare	7	5.8
Construction and real estate	6	5.0
Food and agriculture	6	5.0
Oil and gas	5	4.2
Others	8	6.7

Present Skills and Competencies of Supply Chain Managers

The present skills and competencies expected of supply chain managers are provided in Table 14.

The results indicate that all 10 categories of skills and competencies expected of supply chain managers are relevant ($\bar{X} > 3.5$). However, in terms of relative importance, leadership and decision-making skills are perceived to be the most important category with $\bar{X} = 4.21$, SD = 0.88. This shows the importance of supply chain managers to demonstrate leadership skills (Tantham *et al.*, 2017). As evident during the

Table 14: Present skills and competencies of supply chain managers

Categories and Items	Mean	SD	Item Rank	Category Rank
Leadership and decision–making	**4.21**	**0.88**		1
Leadership skills	4.25	0.85	1	
Decision-making skills	4.17	0.91	6	
Relationship management	**4.06**	**0.94**		2
People skills	4.23	0.91	2	
Negotiation skills	4.17	0.89	5	
Cross-functional coordination skills	3.98	0.92	14	
Team orientation	4.09	0.93	10	
Cross-cultural management	3.79	1.05	33	
Supply chain planning	**4.03**	**0.98**		3
Facilities location planning	3.80	1.07	31	
Production planning	4.07	1.08	11	
Distribution planning	4.23	0.81	3	
General management	**3.96**	**0.98**		4
Time management	4.10	0.93	9	
Project management	3.98	0.96	15	
Risk management	3.96	1.04	16	
Quality management	3.93	1.03	21	
Change management	3.91	0.94	23	
Conflict management	3.88	1.00	28	
Soft skills	**3.95**	**0.92**		5
Oral communication	4.04	0.87	12	
Written communication	3.93	0.89	19	
Documentation and reporting	3.91	1.00	24	
Analytical skills	3.90	1.01		6
Quantitative modelling	3.53	1.07	43	
Data analytics	3.89	1.00	27	
Demand forecasting	4.20	0.99	4	
Costing and budgeting	4.11	0.93	8	
Benchmarking skills	3.78	1.09	34	

Table 14: (*Continued*)

Categories and Items	Mean	SD	Item Rank	Category Rank
Supply chain functional aspects	3.88	0.99		7
Supply chain policies, laws, and regulation	3.78	1.01	35	
Supply chain process mapping/integration	3.93	0.96	20	
Supply chain process reengineering/ optimization	3.84	1.05	30	
Supply chain financing	3.75	1.13	36	
Strategic sourcing/procurement	4.13	0.90	7	
Asset and inventory management	4.01	0.88	13	
Transportation/fleet management	3.95	0.99	17	
Freight management	3.91	1.04	22	
Warehouse management	3.89	1.00	26	
3PL management	3.66	0.99	37	
Supply chain technologies	3.60	1.07		8
E-commerce technologies	3.91	1.02	25	
Enterprise resource planning (ERP) systems	3.79	1.00	32	
E-procurement	3.66	1.03	38	
Supply chain automation	3.50	1.02	44	
Blockchain technology	3.12	1.24	50	
Information technology	3.94	1.00	18	
Artificial intelligence and machine learning	3.34	1.12	49	
Industry 4.0 technologies (in general)	3.58	1.12	41	
Software application	3.59	1.20		9
Software design and development	3.42	1.31	47	
Software programming	3.50	1.26	45	
Software use	3.86	1.04	29	
Sustainability	3.52	1.13		10
Lean tools and methodologies	3.61	1.15	39	
Six sigma tools	3.46	1.10	46	
ISO 14000 standards	3.60	1.16	40	
Reverse logistics	3.58	1.08	42	
Circular economy	3.34	1.15	48	

COVID-19, organizations have relied on their supply chain managers to lead them out of the crisis. Previous studies have mentioned the need for a supply chain manager to be a coach who "teaches, mentors and motivates others to contribute as part of a team," and a champion "who establishes credibility throughout all levels of the organization" (Ellinger and Ellinger, 2014).

Relationship management emerged as the second important category with $\bar{X} = 4.06$, SD = 0.94. This supports the findings of earlier studies that supply chain managers must be relationship managers (Mangan and Christopher, 2005), including strong customer relationship management and supplier relationship management (Dubey and Gunasekaran, 2015; Tantham *et al.*, 2017). Supply chain planning emerged as the third important category with $\bar{X} = 4.03$, SD = 0.98. Previous studies have stressed the importance of supply chain managers moving from a reactive mode to a planning mode in terms of project scoping, goal-setting, and execution (Prajogo and Sohal, 2013). According to APICS (2009), supply chain managers must effectively plan what is to be achieved.

Surprisingly, general management skills and competencies emerged as the fourth important category with $\bar{X} = 3.96$, SD = 0.98 and was perceived to be more important than supply chain functional skills and competencies. Skills and competencies in supply chain functional aspects were ranked only seventh in terms of relative importance with $\bar{X} = 3.88$, SD = 0.99. The results echo the calls in the literature for having generalist, MBA-type programs that prepare supply chain managers for the spatial, temporal, and economic challenges they are increasingly facing as opposed to functionalist educational programs in sub-disciplines of SCM such as procurement and logistics (Tantham *et al.*, 2017). For instance, Ellinger and Ellinger (2014) stressed the need for supply chain managers to be like a choreographer who sees "the big picture while understanding where individual pieces fit the pattern."

Soft skills emerged as the fifth important category with $\bar{X} = 3.95$, SD = 0.92, higher than functional skills and competencies, and hard skills like analytical skills and technological skills. Analytical skills were perceived to be the sixth important category with $\bar{X} = 3.90$, SD = 1.01. The relatively higher SD (>1) shows a varying difference in perceptions across respondents. The results show that SCM is still not just a numbers game. While analytical skills are necessary but creative thinking and the ability to see the big picture are more important for today's supply chain. Surprisingly, despite all the buzz around supply chain technologies, it was only perceived as the eighth important out of the 10 categories with a relatively lower mean score of $\bar{X}$= 3.60, SD = 1.07. Similarly, software application emerged as the second least important skills and competencies $\bar{X}$= 3.59, SD = 1.20. This could well be because of the availability of ready-to-use or plug-and-play software that requires eliminates the need for software design and development and programming. Finally, despite all the recent buzz around sustainability, it emerged as the least important skill and competency for supply chain managers.

The individual item level across all categories is seen in Table 14.

Regarding the top three, leadership skills emerged as the most critical competency of supply chain managers with $\bar{X}$= 4.25, SD = 0.85. This supports the findings of Tantham *et al.* (2017), who found leadership as the most desired competency of supply chain managers, especially during uncertainty. People skill emerged as the second most crucial skill for supply chain managers ($\bar{X}$= 4.23, SD = 0.91). Distribution planning emerged as the third most important competency of supply chain managers with ($\bar{X}$=4.23, SD=0.81). This is not surprising given the increasingly complex distribution network of global supply chains. In terms of the least essential skills and competencies at the individual level, blockchain technology emerged as the least important ($\bar{X}$= 3.12, SD = 1.24). The relatively high SD shows there is a considerable difference in perceptions across supply chain managers. The low score could be because blockchain is a relatively new technology and most of its successful use cases are seen in western countries. Similarly, artificial intelligence and machine learning emerged as the second least important with $\bar{X}$= 3.34, SD = 1.12). Circular economy, despite a lot of interest in recent years, appeared as the third least essential item with $\bar{X}$= 3.34, SD = 1.15.

Future Skills and Competencies of Supply Chain Managers

The future skills and competencies expected of supply chain managers are provided in Table 15.

Table 15: Future skills and competencies of supply chain managers

Categories and Items	M	SD	Item Rank	Category Rank
Leadership and decision-making	**4.50**	**0.78**		1
Leadership skills	4.53	0.75	1	
Decision-making skills	4.47	0.81	3	
Relationship management	**4.30**	**0.86**		2
People skills	4.43	0.82	4	
Negotiation skills	4.34	0.79	10	
Cross-functional coordination skills	4.31	0.86	14	
Team orientation	4.30	0.87	16	
Cross-cultural management	4.13	0.95	29	
General management	**4.24**	**0.89**		3
Time management	4.40	0.89	6	
Project management	4.14	0.89	27	
Risk management	4.37	0.86	8	
Quality management	4.22	0.93	22	
Change management	4.22	0.82	23	
Conflict management	4.08	0.92	31	
Analytical skills	**4.23**	**0.88**		4
Quantitative modeling	3.97	0.94	41	
Data analytics	4.40	0.86	5	
Demand forecasting	4.48	0.82	2	
Costing and budgeting	4.34	0.80	11	
Benchmarking skills	3.98	0.99	40	
Supply chain planning	**4.22**	**0.97**		5
Facilities location planning	4.07	1.09	32	
Production planning	4.20	1.01	25	
Distribution planning	4.39	0.80	7	
Supply chain technologies	**4.19**	**0.96**		6
E-commerce technologies	4.36	0.87	9	
Enterprise resource planning (ERP) systems	4.00	1.04	39	
E-Procurement	4.24	0.93	21	
Supply chain automation	4.28	0.91	18	

Table 15: (*Continued*)

Categories and Items	M	SD	Item Rank	Category Rank
Blockchain technology	3.84	1.17	45	
Information technology	4.32	0.91	13	
Artificial intelligence and machine learning	4.19	0.99	26	
Industry 4.0 technologies (in general)	4.29	0.85	17	
Soft skills	**4.13**	**0.94**		7
Oral communication	4.31	0.88	15	
Written communication	4.13	0.94	28	
Documentation and reporting	3.95	1.00	42	
Supply chain functional aspects	4.09	0.95		8
Supply chain policies, laws, and regulation	4.10	0.92	30	
Supply chain process mapping/ integration	4.27	0.89	20	
Supply chain process reengineering/ optimization	4.21	0.93	24	
Supply chain financing	4.03	0.93	35	
Strategic sourcing/procurement	4.34	0.86	12	
Asset and inventory management	4.01	0.96	37	
Transportation/fleet management	4.05	1.00	33	
Freight management	4.03	1.01	34	
Warehouse management	4.02	1.00	36	
3PL management	3.86	1.02	44	
Software Application	**3.96**	**1.14**		9
Software design and development	3.78	1.22	48	
Software programming	3.83	1.22	46	
Software use	4.28	0.97	19	
Sustainability	**3.81**	**1.10**		10
Lean tools and methodologies	3.88	1.06	43	
Six sigma tools	3.64	1.07	50	
ISO 14000 standards	3.70	1.17	49	
Reverse logistics	4.00	1.10	38	
Circular economy	3.82	1.11	47	

The results indicate that all 10 categories of skills and competencies expected of supply chain managers are expected to be more relevant in the future ($\bar{X} > 3.8$), although the relative importance of some of the categories has changed for the future. However, leadership and decision-making skills are still the most important category for future supply chain managers with $\bar{X} = 4.50$, SD = 0.78. Even in the future, relationship management will remain the second most important category with $\bar{X} = 4.30$, SD = 0.80. General management skills and competencies are perceived to be even more critical for the future vis-à-vis present, as it is ranked as the third most important category in the future with $\bar{X} = 4.24$, SD = 0.89. On the contrary, the relevance of supply chain functional skills and competencies dropped even further to eighth place with $\bar{X} = 4.09$, SD = 0.95. This further emphasizes the need for a generalist instead of a functionalist approach in managing future supply chains.

The need for supply chain managers to possess analytical skills is much more significant in the future. Compared to the present scenario, it has improved its ranking significantly from sixth to fourth most essential skills and competencies for supply chain managers with $\bar{X} = 4.23$, SD = 0.88. In other words, SCM will become more of a numbers game in the future. This is not surprising given the advancements in big data and advanced modeling techniques to improve decision-making for all activities across the supply chain. Although the perceived importance of supply chain planning has been enhanced to $\bar{X} = 4.22$, SD = 0.97, its ranking has dropped two places to fifth in the relative importance of supply skills and competencies. On the other hand, supply chain technologies have improved two places to move to sixth in the order of importance. This is not surprising, given that advanced technology will increasingly be used to improve transparency and visibility throughout the supply chain network (Oracle, 2021). On the other hand, soft skills have dropped two places to seventh in relative importance for the future with $\bar{X} = 4.13$, SD = 0.94. While this does not undermine the importance of soft skills, the results show that supply managers need to emphasize more on hard skills such as technology and analytics. Skills and competencies related to software application were perceived to be higher in the future ($\bar{X} = 3.96$, SD = 1.14), although it remained in the ninth position. The need for a sustainability mindset and associated skills and competencies also was perceived to be higher in the future with $\bar{X}$= 3.81, SD = 1.10. However, in terms of its ranking, it still remains the least essential skills and competencies expected of supply chain managers. This is surprising given that supply chains are considered a game-changer in the fight against climate change. There is increasing pressure on supply chains and supply chain managers to reduce their environmental footprint.

In terms of individual items, leadership skills have retained their top position as the most critical competency for supply chain managers in the future with $\bar{X}$= 4.50, SD = 0.78, while the second and third most crucial skill set and competencies have changed for future supply chain managers. Demand forecasting, a classical skill requirement of supply chain managers, emerged as the second most important skill for supply chain managers. Compared to the current scenario, its ranking has improved two places in the ranking with $\bar{X}$= 4.48, SD = 0.82. Decision-making skills moved three places to third with $\bar{X}$=4.48, SD=0.81. This shows that future supply chain managers must develop the capability to, in quick time, take the lead in critical decisions, especially during uncertainty. Software design and development ($\bar{X}$= 3.78, SD = 1.22), ISO 14001 standards ($\bar{X}$= 3.70, SD = 1.17), and six sigma tools ($\bar{X}$= 3.64, SD = 1.07) emerged as the least three essential skills and competencies in the future. As mentioned earlier, the lower importance of software design and development is likely because of the readily available software, eliminating the need for in-house software development. For ISO 14001 and six sigma tools, supply chain managers may consider these standards and tools less significant or even obsolete in the future.

Present and Future Skills and Competency Gap for Supply Chain Managers

In line with research question 3 (see page 80), the study computed the mean difference in the present and future skills and competencies at the category and individual levels. The results are provided in Table 16 (category level) and Table 17 (individual level).

Table 16: Present and future skill and competency gap the category level

Categories and Items	Mean (Present)	Mean (Future)	Mean Difference (δ)
Supply chain technologies	3.60	4.19	0.59***
Software application	3.59	3.96	0.37***
Analytical skills	3.90	4.23	0.33***
Sustainability	3.52	3.81	0.29***
Leadership and decision-making	4.21	4.50	0.29***
General management	3.96	4.24	0.28***
Relationship management	4.06	4.30	0.24***
Supply chain functional aspects	3.88	4.09	0.21***
Supply chain planning	4.03	4.22	0.19**
Soft skills	3.95	4.13	0.18**

***Significant at $p < 0.001$; $p < 0.01$.

Table 17: Present and future skill and competency gap at the individual level

Categories and Items	Mean (Present)	Mean (Future)	Mean Difference (δ)
Artificial intelligence and machine learning	3.34	4.19	0.85
Supply chain automation	3.50	4.28	0.78
Blockchain technology	3.12	3.84	0.72
Industry 4.0 technologies (in general)	3.58	4.29	0.71
E-procurement	3.66	4.24	0.58
Data analytics	3.89	4.40	0.51
Circular economy	3.34	3.82	0.48
E-commerce technologies	3.91	4.36	0.45
Quantitative modeling	3.53	3.97	0.44
Software use	3.86	4.28	0.42
Reverse logistics	3.58	4.00	0.42
Risk management	3.96	4.37	0.41
Information technology	3.94	4.32	0.38
Supply chain process reengineering/ optimization	3.84	4.21	0.37

Table 17: (*Continued*)

Categories and Items	Mean (Present)	Mean (Future)	Mean Difference (δ)
Software design and development	3.42	3.78	0.36
Cross-cultural management	3.79	4.13	0.34
Supply chain process mapping/ Integration	3.93	4.27	0.34
Software programming	3.50	3.83	0.33
Cross-functional coordination skills	3.98	4.31	0.33
Supply chain policies, laws, and regulation	3.78	4.10	0.32
Change management	3.91	4.22	0.31
Time management	4.10	4.40	0.30
Decision-making skills	4.17	4.47	0.30
Quality management	3.93	4.22	0.29
Supply chain financing	3.75	4.03	0.28
Demand forecasting	4.20	4.48	0.28
Leadership skills	4.25	4.53	0.28
Facilities location planning	3.80	4.07	0.27
Lean tools and methodologies	3.61	3.88	0.27
Oral communication	4.04	4.31	0.27
Costing and budgeting	4.11	4.34	0.23
Strategic sourcing/procurement	4.13	4.34	0.21
Enterprise resource planning (ERP) systems	3.79	4.00	0.21
Team orientation	4.09	4.30	0.21
Benchmarking skills	3.78	3.98	0.20
Conflict management	3.88	4.08	0.20
3PL management	3.66	3.86	0.20
Written communication	3.93	4.13	0.20
People skills	4.23	4.43	0.20
Six sigma tools	3.46	3.64	0.18
Negotiation skills	4.17	4.34	0.17
Project management	3.98	4.14	0.16
Distribution planning	4.23	4.39	0.16

(*Continued*)

Table 17: (*Continued*)

Categories and Items	Mean (Present)	Mean (Future)	Mean Difference (δ)
Production planning	4.07	4.20	0.13
Warehouse management	3.89	4.02	0.13
Freight management	3.91	4.03	0.12
ISO 14000 standards	3.60	3.70	0.10
Transportation/fleet management	3.95	4.05	0.10
Documentation and reporting	3.91	3.95	0.04
Asset and inventory management	4.01	4.01	0.00

As seen in Table 16, at the category level, the present and future skill and competency gaps are evident for all categories. Moreover, paired *t*-test results for the present and future show the difference is significant. The gap is highest for supply chain technologies ($\delta = 0.59$, $p < 0.001$). This was followed by a software application ($\delta = 0.37$, $p < 0.001$) and analytical skills ($\delta = 0.33$, $p < 0.001$). In other words, the top three gap categories represent hard skills. As mentioned earlier, future supply chain managers must possess hard technical skills along with soft skills. There is also a significant gap in the sustainability skills and competencies ($\delta = 0.29$, $p < 0.001$), leadership skills and competencies ($\delta = 0.29$, $p < 0.001$), and general management skills and competencies ($\delta = 0.28$, $p < 0.001$). Addressing these skills and competency gaps of supply chain managers is critical for the effective management of future supply chains. The skill gap was found to be relatively low of relationship management ($\delta = 0.24$, $p < 0.001$), supply chain functional aspects ($\delta = 0.21$, $p < 0.001$), supply chain planning ($\delta = 0.21$, $p < 0.01$), and soft skills ($\delta = 0.18$, $p < 0.01$).

The present and future skill and competency gaps at the individual level are given in Table 17.

As seen in Table 17, the top five gaps in skills and competencies appear in supply chain technologies. The gap is highest for artificial intelligence and machine learning ($\delta = 0.85$). This was followed by supply chain automation ($\delta = 0.78$), blockchain technology ($\delta = 0.72$), and Industry 4.0 technologies in general ($\delta = 0.71$). The results are not surprising, given that adoption of Industry 4.0 technologies such as AI, machine learning, the IoT, automation, and sensors in the supply chain will be greater in the future and will transform the way companies manufacture, maintain, and distribute new products and services (Oracle, 2021). Also, E-procurement ($\delta = 0.58$) and E-commerce technologies ($\delta = 0.45$) featured in the top ten skill and competency gap. In terms of analytical skills, data analytics ($\delta = 0.51$) and quantitative modeling ($\delta = 0.44$) are also featured in the top 10 skills and competency gaps. The only sustainability aspect featured in the top 10 skill and competency gap is the awareness and knowledge of the "circular economy" concept. This is likely because of the recent push towards building a circular supply chain to eliminate waste and create a closed-loop system through reuse, sharing, repair, refurbishment, remanufacturing, and recycling to minimize resource inputs and reduce waste, pollution, and carbon emissions (Forbes, 2021). On the other hand, skill gap was found to be least for supply chain functional skills such as warehouse management ($\delta = 0.13$), freight management ($\delta = 0.12$), transportation/fleet management ($\delta = 0.10$), and asset and inventory management ($\delta = 0.00$) in addition to ISO 14001 standards ($\delta = 0.10$), and documentation and reporting ($\delta = 0.04$).

Discussion

In line with the research questions, the study identified the present and future skills and competencies of supply chain managers. A total of 50 important skills and competencies across ten categories were first identified from the literature. Through a structured survey of supply chain managers, the relative importance of present and future supply chain skills and competencies expected of supply chain managers in Asia was understood. In addition, gap analysis and paired sample *t*-test were employed to identify the present and future skill and competency gap. The results show that supply chain managers must demonstrate multidimensional skills and competencies. Leadership and relationship management skills and competencies remain the two most essential skills and competencies for supply chain managers for the present and future. Organizations, therefore, must strive to provide leadership training and relationship management training such as on people management skills, negotiation skills, cross-cultural, and cross-functional management skills.

Moreover, besides the classical functional supply chain expertise such as warehouse management and transportation management, supply chain managers of present and future need to demonstrate even greater generalist competencies covering risk management, project management, quality management, change management, and time management. Similarly, besides soft skills, future supply chain managers are expected to possess hard skills such as technological and analytical skills. The findings overall provide a road map for organizations and educators looking to develop the essential skills and competencies of supply chain managers for managing the present and future supply chains. It also enables organizations to make changes in their hiring, training, and retention strategies of supply chain managers. While the study was conducted in Asia, for future researchers, the supply chain skills and competencies listed in this study and their categorization can be employed in different settings.

Chapter 5

Summary from the Interviews, Survey, and Job Postings

Introduction

This research has several academic implications. First of all, it helps to enrich the contemporary literature on competency and skill sets for supply chain managers in Asia, which is currently limited. Second, this study involves online survey, job postings, and one-to-one interview with senior managers which help to validate the data using triangulation method. Findings from this research also indicate the consistency in findings from several earlier studies in the field, while also discovering that new skills and knowledge during the pandemic which are critical for supply chain professionals. Table 18 shows the summary results from the three studies.

The results from the survey have shown that supply chain managers must demonstrate multidimensional skills and competencies. Leadership and relationship management skills and competencies remain the two most essential skills and competencies for supply chain managers for the present and future. Organizations, therefore, must strive to provide leadership training and relationship management training such as on people management skills, negotiation skills, cross-cultural, and cross-functional management skills.

Moreover, besides the classical functional supply chain expertise such as warehouse management and transportation management, supply chain managers of present and future need to demonstrate even greater generalist competencies covering risk management, project

Table 18: Summary from the three research methods

Research Method	Interviews	Online Job Posting	Survey
Key skills	Data analysis	Supply chain analytical	Leadership and Decision making
Key skills	Software application	Technological aptitude	Relationship management
Key skills	Soft skills	Teamwork skills	Supply chain planning
Future skills	Technology automation	Nil	Leadership and decision-making
Future skills	Collaboration	Nil	Relationship management
Future skills	Customer oriented	Nil	General management

management, quality management, change management, and time management. Similarly, besides soft skills, future supply chain managers are expected to possess hard skills such as technological and analytical skills. The findings overall provide a road map for organizations and educators looking to develop the essential skills and competencies of supply chain managers for managing the present and future supply chains. It also enables organizations to make changes in their hiring, training, and retention strategies of supply chain managers. While the study was conducted in Asia, for future researchers, the supply chain skills and competencies listed in this study and their categorization can be employed in different settings.

Analytical skills, technological aptitude, teamwork skills, customer-oriented, and leadership skills are all common skills sought by businesses in the logistics and supply chain professions based on interviews with senior managers and from the job postings. Employers are looking for well-rounded employees with superior soft and hard skills based in the job posting.

With globalization, increased product complexity, and heightened customer demands, companies are taking up advanced technologies to transform their supply chain from a pure operations hub into the epicenter of business innovation according to the interviewees. Using sensors and ever-improving internet connectivity, forward-thinking companies are collecting data at every checkpoint, from the status of raw materials flow to the condition and location of finished goods. Machine learning, artificial intelligence (AI), and advanced analytics help drive automation and deliver insights that promote efficiencies — making on-the-fly route changes to accelerate product delivery, for example, or swapping out materials to take advantage of better pricing or availability. 3D printing allows firms to localize production of goods closer to customers, allowing for faster turnaround, reduced transportation costs, and greater personalization. Additive manufacturing is also opening doors to easy production of spare parts, enabling companies to slash inventory, cut costs, and create supplementary revenue streams.

These advanced technologies are serving as a springboard for new business models — for example, many firms are piggybacking off the "internet of things" (IoT) to offer predictive maintenance services that guarantee product uptime while generating recurring revenue. Supply chain professionals are expected to understand how these advanced technologies work and leverage on them to compete more effectively. These advanced technologies can provide them with better tools for decision-making and optimize their resources.

In fact, the top five gaps in skills and competencies from the survey and interviews are the abilities to understand and deploy supply chain technologies. The gap is highest for artificial intelligence and machine learning, followed by supply chain automation, blockchain technology, and Industry 4.0 technologies. The results are not surprising, given that adoption of Industry 4.0 technologies such as AI, machine learning, the IoT, automation, and sensors in the supply chain will be of greater importance in the future and will transform the way companies manufacture, maintain, and distribute new products and services (Oracle, 2021). In terms of analytical skills, data analytics and quantitative modeling are also featured in the top ten skills and competency gaps.

This information is beneficiary to human resource managers for their new hires, while policy makers and educational and training bodies can also use the findings from this research to design new courses which are necessary to facilitate skill and knowledge development for the future supply chain professionals.

Interviewees have also indicated the need to be more resilient supply chains to ensure that they can continue production in the face of any challenge. A good supply chain resilience strategy has three core enablers: people, process, and technology. Employees do their best work when they are empowered by effective, robust processes. To manage component shortages and obsolescence and to increase supply chain resilience, companies need to bolster their processes in the following areas:

Processes that Companies Need to Excel for Supply Chain Resilience

Forecasting

Some of the interviewees have indicated the need to sharpen forecasting skills. This helps secure supply with good information. Then, think about what you need in the long term. If you start ordering parts two weeks before they are needed (because you didn't forecast effectively), you will have a very low chance of procuring what you need in time. But, knowing in advance that you have demand in the pipeline from good forecasting, you may have time to secure supply and stay ahead of shortages.

To drive a robust forecasting process, you need to link sales requirements to operations, raw materials, and component availability. In the past, sales and operations planning (S&OP) has resembled a "load and chase" process as companies made decisions in silos with disconnected tools. This time-consuming and reactive approach has resulted in an excess of materials and capacity. However, an integrated S&OP allows realistic, feasible, and flexible planning with trade-off analysis. Overall, it is a more efficient and proactive approach to SCM.

Inventory Management

Most of the interviewees from trading and retailing believe inventory management is critical today, add safety stock to reduce the risk of a production slow down or halt. Also, focus on supply assurance versus shortage management. Shortage management is a strategy that looks at how many of a specific item is needed by a specific date and guides purchasing managers to procure based on this information. Supply assurance looks at all the needed parts over a very long horizon, taking into account possible shortages and obsolescence, and develops supply plans for those parts.

Companies should invest in optimized inventory strategies to drive order flexibility and service level performance. These include managing long lead times, inventory positioning, safety stock to counter unexpected demands and dynamic, localized replenishment models to ensure materials are delivered exactly when they are needed — not simply when they are forecasted to be needed.

Supplier Relationships and Sourcing

Interviewees from the logistics industry have indicated to develop better relationship with the clients. Make sure you have a good reason for working with specific suppliers and customers. Stay away from single-source relationships and work to expand your supply network. Develop a second source relationship and define geographic priorities to reduce supply chain risk. That said, there are times when companies have to rely on a single source relationship as a result of cost, technology, or other factors. Developing a solid supplier–customer relationship takes time and it is usually best to start building this relationship in a balanced market. Then, when the market turns, your supplier base or partner should return the favor and help you procure the items you need.

Chapter 6

Recommendations

Introduction

This research started with a survey questionnaire that was divided into three skill categories, namely supply chain competency group, managerial competency group, and IT competency group. Both quantitative and qualitative studies have shown significant correlations for the development of a Supply Chain Leadership Framework. Murphy and Poist (1991b) identified the following skillsets and qualifications needed for senior-level managers in companies:

- Business skills
- Logistics skills
- Management skills

The APICS Supply Chain Council (APICS SCC) has identified seven core competencies as essential for leadership success in the supply chain (Marino Donati, Procurement, August 18, 2015):

1. Creating and communicating a vision
2. Promoting and bringing about change
3. Building partnerships
4. Capturing and acting on insightful information
5. Seizing and creating opportunities at the right place and time
6. Consistently modeling honorable behavior and best practices
7. Serving the best interests of the organization without being self-serving

These and many other studies are useful content in search of a Supply Chain Leadership Competency Framework. In view of Industry 4.0 transformation, the supply chain sustainability is under the watchful eyes of business owners and C-level senior executives to prepare future generations of supply chain leaders that possess the right competencies, skillsets, technologies, and management capabilities to bring the value chain integration and optimization to the new level.

Supply Chain Leadership Framework

The authors propose a SCM 3P Leadership Competency Framework, namely, People, Process, and Practices. The key competencies for People are Communication, Coordination, and Collaboration. These are multidisciplinary skillsets covering Business skills, Management skills, and Logistics skills. The key competencies for Process are Empathy, Engagement, and Employability. From Table 18, summary from the three research methods, in order to be able to have good relationship management, team management, and both intra- and interorganizational engagement, SCM leaders must possess empathy to start with. Strong SCM leadership demands rigorous engagement process to deal with both internal and external stakeholders. With strong SCM leadership, employee or staff employability is sustained. Gallup studies show that organizations that are focusing on strengths in their people are six times more engaging than those that are not; their employees enjoy three times higher quality of work life. Because of improved employee engagement, organizations enjoy increase of Return on Investments (ROI), Productivity, Engagement, and Customer Impact. Because of improvement in quality of work life, there is decrease in sick leaves, staff turnover, conflicts, and accidents at work. The key competencies for Practices are Define, Develop, and Deliver. Practices through IoT, artificial intelligence, and deep technologies using blockchains to optimize inventory management and flows, and FinTech platforms that provide seamless, cashless, and rapid, efficient fiscal transactions. The traditional SCM Leadership Competency Framework provides a conventional perspective of SCM Leadership that perpetuates with educational curriculum in SCM courses and

Table 19: Supply chain management 3P leadership competency framework

3Ps		Entry	Experienced	Expert
People	***Communication Coordination Collaboration***	Introductory soft skills to interpersonal interactions and creation of synergy	Advanced and current soft skills to interpersonal interactions and creation of synergy	Progressive and strategic soft skills to interpersonal interactions and creation of synergy
Process	***Empathy Engagement Employability***	Basic interpersonal relationship building, engagement, and sustainable roadmap	Advanced and current interpersonal relationship building, engagement, and sustainable roadmap	Progressive and strategic interpersonal relationship building, engagement, and sustainable roadmap
Practice	***Define Develop Deliver***	Fundamental SCM knowledge and skillsets applying technologies	Advanced and current SCM knowledge and skillsets applying technologies	Progressive and strategic SCM knowledge and skillsets applying technologies

academic discourses of strategic SCM Leadership that often turn out to be another perfunctory exercise. In the proposed SCM Leadership Competency Framework as illustrated in Table 19, the 3Ps form the vertical columns and the three tiers of SCM competencies form the horizontal rows. The details of this SCM 3P Leadership Competency Framework are discussed in subsequent sections.

In the 1980s, Dr Michael Hammer propounded Business Process Reengineering (Michael Hammer, 1990) and defined "Reengineering is the radical redesign of business processes for dramatic improvement." He started by looking at "radical" redesign as the key to reengineering. There was a need to create value for what we engaged in. He thought the radical redesign of processes will achieve that end goal. Overtime, Dr Hammer rediscovered that the key to successful reengineering was not the word "radical," but "process!" A complete end-to-end set of activities that together create value for customers. However, processes alone can only drive improvements as they are originally designed for. Ultimately, it is the "people" element that makes things thick in a dynamic fashion. The Business Process Reengineering (BPR) Framework as described by Dr Hammer:

a. Vision and mission
b. Business process
c. Current technologies
d. People driver

Hence, in the proposed SCM 3P Leadership Competency Framework, people is key to an established leadership competency framework. Without People, there is no Leader! Process and Practices can't lead ... it is People that leads!

People Domain

The *homo sapiens* of the new millennium is blessed with advanced technologies. People are spoilt for choices to technology deployment. However, the dynamic nature of People is constantly influenced and surrounded by VUCA (Volatility, Uncertainty, Complexity, Ambiguity). The VUCA world is hostile and unforgiving to the people of this generation. The three competencies for People domain to develop are: Communication, Coordination, and Collaboration. There is a need to transpose VUCA to VUCA+ (plus). Instead of Volatility, people need to be guided by Vision which coincides with the first element of the BPR framework. A vision provides a strategic goal, a corporate target, and the expected outcome of a business. Without a clear Vision, the corporation perishes! One of the first step to establish SCM Leadership Competency Framework is to establish clearly documented Vision for the organization.

Once the Vision is established, People need to transpose Uncertainty to Understanding. This is where communication plays a huge role in interpersonal relationship building. Not only communication, but effective communication is greatly needed. Communication is like breathing to the human lungs. We cannot communicate. When people don't communicate, there is no relationship. Typically, when people are in conflict, communication stops. This will be a great hindrance to SCM. Conflict resolution begins with getting people to communicate again, and communication engenders understanding.

Next is to transpose Complexity to Clarity. Clear vision and mission are the starting point to create understanding and thus progress. Clarity of standard operations procedures (SOP) helps to move things efficiently and effectiveness. Clarity of strategic SCM processes provides the efficacy for long-term SCM sustainability and to achieve quantum leap outcome. The clear vision and understanding connect value chains and create a smooth process for synergistic partnerships. This is needed for the second and third SCM Leadership Competency in the People domain, namely, Coordination and Collaboration.

Finally, from Ambiguity to Agility! Much confusion and miscommunication attribute to ambiguities. Ambiguity is the devil that cooks up the storm. Ambiguity is a sign of noncommitment, it breaks trust and creates not only distrust and uncertainty, it also haunts the business partnership into cold war, and potentially business failures. Business partnership needs strategic level of agility to lubricate the relationship and hone the level of trust between people. Agility offers dynamic flexibility and adaptability. Agility is about speed and trust. Agility provides speedy win–win conflict resolution when one appears. Agility provides repeatability of solutions that engenders great long-term business partnerships.

In summary, the new millennium approach is the transpose VUCA to VUCA+:

a. Volatility to vision
b. Uncertainty to understanding
c. Complexity to clarity
d. Ambiguity to agility

The new millennium SCM Leaders need to operate in VUCA+ ambience. Developing competencies in Communication, Coordination, and Collaboration.

In SCM, coordination is seen as operational skillset. More than that, coordination is a people competency is greatly needed to ensure sustainable and smooth supply chain operations. The ability for SCM leader to coordinate supply chain processes well, starts with effective communication. Coordination takes place when effective communication takes place between parties in the supply chain. Effective coordination is the outcome of effective communication. Effective communication and effective coordination lead to effective collaboration.

In Dr Stephen Covey's highly famed book *Seven Habits of Highly Effective People*, the sixth habit is Synergy. Synergy is simply described as one plus one is greater than two. Greek philosopher Aristotle said, "The whole is more powerful than the sum of the individuals." This is Synergy. People need each other; no one is an island. The key to a collaborative business partnership stands from the possession of personal leadership and corporate leadership. Dr Covey's seven habits are:

Habit 1: Be proactive
Habit 2: Begin with the end in mind
Habit 3: Put first things first
Habit 4: Think win–win
Habit 5: Seek first to understand then to be understood
Habit 6: Synergy
Habit 7: Sharpen the saw

Habits 1 to 3 are about personal leadership. Every SCM leader should practice these personal leadership habits daily. Be proactive, begin with the end in mind, put first things first, help to build SCM leadership competencies in engaging the outside world.

Habits 4 to 6 are about corporate leadership and team leadership. Dr Covey emphasized either "win–win" or no deal. The SCM leader must be clear that that's no compromise in the SCM but only win–win business relationships that will help them to build reputation and sustainable SCM leadership.

Habit 7 is what the Japanese call "Kaizen" or continuous improvement. SCM leadership competency is a continuum. Starting with the Entry tier, to the Experienced tier, and finally to the Expert tier, SCM leaders continue to mature and grow into a sustainable SCM leadership status. In the SCM 3P Leadership Competency Framework context, personal leadership continues with the corporate leadership. People lead people. The strategic development of the People competency puts the SCM leaders in good stake and well positioned to provide leadership not only to their own organization but also to the entire value chain concerned.

In the 1990s, it was an era for supply chain optimization. In order to achieve supply chain optimization, SCM leaders rely on data and systems integration to manage their logistics pull and push. For several years, the focus was technology and application integration. How an organization integrates the ERP systems and their office automation applications became prime focus. Behind all the systems integration and applications connectivity lies on the people competency. The typical systems implementation calls for the need to help end users to overcome the resistance to change. Those were the days when senior operators refuse to use the keyboards or have difficulty carrying out data entry accurately. And there were pushbacks on using computer systems, especially web-based systems. The lack of familiarity and confidence in conducting the use of technology create resistance, fear of failures, and poor performance. Hence, the challenge was not with systems integration but with people competency. There was a need for paradigm shifts. Hence, IT practitioners and ERP consultants introduced barcoding, RFID, and today, QR codes to ease the systems implementation challenges. Once again, it is people competency that requires to "sharpen the saw" (Dr Stephen Covey's Habit number 7).

When SCM leaders acquire all three competencies in the People domain, namely, Communication, Coordination, and Collaboration, they gain the skillsets and experiences to empathize, engage, and employ SCM practitioners throughout the value chains. Table 19 illustrates the three tiers of People domain: Introduction (Entry), Advanced and Current (Experienced), and Progressive and Strategic (Expert) tiers. In order to measure these competency achievements, key performance indicators (KPIs) are meted out to each tier from one tier to another.

Companies need enough manpower to complete the work, but they also need skilled workers with the knowledge to help their employers tackle tough challenges. Scout for knowledgeable engineers, procurement specialists, and supply chain managers who can supplement existing talent and help the company navigate a difficult business environment. Concurrently, look for people with market knowledge, who can help the company stay ahead of market trends. Manufacturing will never slow down, so you need the right people to help you keep up with the pace of business.

Supplier relationship managers work with a long-term technology roadmap. These individuals do not handle price negotiations or the short-term business of their commodity counterparts. Instead, they are focused on building relationships with suppliers at the executive level by understanding their core business strategies and proactively approaching these partners with opportunities for mutual benefit.

Unfortunately, the COVID-19 pandemic has complicated supplier relationship management. Before the pandemic, supplier relationships relied heavily on face-to-face interactions and in-person meetings. However, travel restrictions are creating a new virtual environment as supply chain professionals conduct their discussions without traveling. This inability to travel builds uncertainty, especially with companies that have been maintaining numerous supplier relationships over many years. Supply chain managers are having to rethink how they can maintain those relationships in a new way. This is especially crucial since supply chain, at its core, is a people business. If a supplier is only running at 20% or 30% capacity because of a disruption, you can bet their limited goods will be prioritized by the strength of their relationships.

Thus, supply chain professionals would need to "think out of the box" to minimize the risk of their companies being ill-prepared for another event with such devastating supply chain consequences. Ideation and scenario-building skills would help them to anticipate the wider ramification of supply chain disruptions such as those caused by COVID-19. The ability to model changing risk profiles during the course of a crisis would also be an asset, particularly where, as with a pandemic, it can last for many months or years.

Many of the interviewees had found it difficult to manage virtual teams during the pandemic and would welcome training in how to do this effectively, drawing on the wide experience that has been gained over the past two years. As hybrid working is now the norm for many people in supply chain and logistics roles, the capability to manage virtual and mixed teams is becoming a core competence. In many cases this will involve increasing managers' digital literacy with online networking tools. So, there are both leadership and technical dimensions to their upskilling for the post-pandemic work environment. At a more fundamental level, the pandemic has demonstrated the need for supply chain managers to factor risk management and resilience into all aspects and levels of their decision-making. This may prove to be its legacy to the SCM profession, preparing it not just for future health crises but for a broad range of other high-impact low-probability events.

Process Domain

The second SCM leadership competency is process domain. Mustering SCM processes is critical in SCM leadership. Understanding supply chain processes is the beginning of SCM. Up to now, we have taken the term SCM for granted without a proper definition. SCM is the management of the flow of goods and services and includes all processes that transform raw materials into final products. It involves the active streamlining of a business's supply-side activities to maximize customer value and gain a competitive advantage in the marketplace. IBM's supply chain practice defines SCM as the handling of the entire production flow of a good or service to maximize quality, delivery, customer experience, and profitability. The key is SCM is really the management of the supply chain. In the marketplace, there are different value chains in operation. On the supply side are the raw materials suppliers, components suppliers, and services suppliers. On the demand side, it is Customer. The entire supply chain push and pull products and services to fulfil customers' demands and needs. The SCM's KPIs lie in customers' satisfaction in terms of the goods and services consumed to the level of satisfaction previously agreed known as the acceptable quality level or more formally acceptance quality limit (AQL). The end consumers' AQL can vary dynamically. Therefore, to achieve SCM success is a perennial problem for SCM leaders. The truth is many SCM leaders are not conversant with SCM processes, and hence fail SCM KPI. We need to address SCM leaders' process competency posthaste.

Table 19 illustrates the three areas of Practice competency: Empathy, Engagement, and Employability.

Empathy

To acquire the Process competency, it begins with Empathy. In the Design Thinking process as illustrated in Figure 4, empathy is the first step in the entire Design Thinking process.

SCM leaders acquire the process competency by first acquiring empathy. Learning to put oneself into the customers' position is the ability to understand the customer pain points and supply chain needs. Only then can SCM leaders define, ideate, prototype, and test supply chain solutions to achieve the supply chain KPIs. The SCM leader's process competency begins with empathy.

If SCM leaders want to achieve SCM success, one key initiative is understanding the developing supply chain processes with the AQL designed into them. The principle behind this is what we want to achieve in the process outcome, we must first design the AQL into the process. What is not incorporated in the process will never be achieved. There is a practitioner mantra to observe: "He who fails to plan, plans to fail." What is not planned for will not take effect. Whatever the AQL

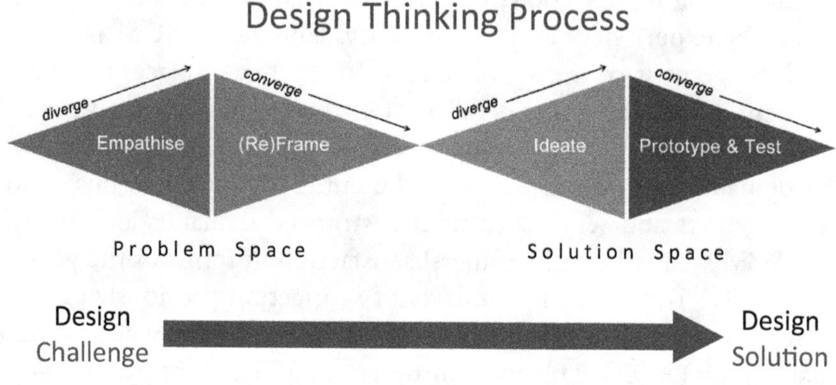

Figure 4: Design thinking process

committed should be designed into the process so that the outcome will be the expected KPI.

One of the approaches in Lean Manufacturing is the remove waste from each process by doing a Value Stream Mapping exercise. The entire supply chain may be considered as one huge value stream mapping. Lean practitioners may walk through the entire supply chain processes with the SCM leader to determine how the supply chain may be optimized by removing those non-value-added activities. Knowing the supply chain processes, understanding the AQL and designed the KPI into each process will ensure that SCM leaders achieve the SCM KPI in the overall supply chain management.

Engagement

Process competency extends beyond Empathy. The ability to interact with customers (both internal and external) is known as Engagement. As mentioned, Gallup's strengths-based approach enables organizations to improve their employee engagement to achieve six times productivity improvement and three times improvement of quality of work life. Engagement is a KPI for Process competency. Every one is gifted with natural talents. Gallup defines talent as the natural recurring patterns of one's thinking, feeling, and behaving. There are 34 talent themes as described by CliftonStrengths assessment. To achieve strengths, one begins with talents. Talents are like raw muscles that require regular exercising to gain strengths. Deploying the Gallup talent framework: Name It-Claim It-Aim It! One starts to understand oneself before attempting to engage with others. The reason is that one sees others through the filter of their own talent lenses. Hence, it is important to know one's talents in order to engage with others effectively.

Employability

The third element in Process competency is Employability. The best way to define Employability is being "usable" according to the English Dictionary. The capability for one who is able to hold a job and available for hire. In the SCM Leadership Competency Framework, Employability represents the SCM leader's contribution to the supply chain community and the organizations concerned. As the SCM leadership competency is a maturity continuum, one's Employability should be sustainable, ready and available whenever being called upon to perform. The SCM leadership is a profession, not just a job to be completed. There is a higher calling beyond fulfilling the job description of the SCM Manager/Director. Table 19 illustrates three tiers of SCM Leadership: Entry, Experienced, and Expert tier.

At the entry tier, the SCM leader acquires Basic interpersonal relationship building, engagement, and sustainable roadmap. Alongside, Empathy and Engagement, the SCM leader enjoys Employability through their contribution to the supply chain processes and supply chain community. Overtime, the SCM leader becomes recognized for their contributions and gain respect and rewards for their contribution. These may be in the form of promotion, or even external engagements with headhunters regularly knocking at their doors for bigger jobs and higher SCM positions. The SCM professionals can become an evergreen profession. As long as there is supply-and-demand, there is supply chain. As long as there are products and services, and customer demands, there will exist a vibrant supply chain for SCM leaders to manage.

Practice Domain

The third SCM leadership competency is practice domain. By and large, this is one most focused SCM leadership competency by SCM leaders. HRM practitioners and SCM practitioners focus their hiring process looking for people largely who are well-versed in supply chain practices. Those with glorious supply chain practice knowledge and experiences have upper hands in the hiring process. Succession planning also ranks supply chain practices as key qualifying criteria in their consideration to promote certain SCM leaders into senior positions. But what exactly are supply chain practices which are relevant today?

From the interviews, supply chain practices focus on the knowledge of materials management, transportation, and warehousing logistics. In today's SCM, the skillsets and knowledge go beyond merely SCM modules in the logistics textbooks. We are crowded by new technologies with the use of IoT, artificial intelligence and deep technologies, supply chain blockchains implementation, and heuristics, which are the order of today. Table 19 illustrates the three areas of Practice competency: Define, Develop, and Deliver.

Define

The supply chain involves multi-transactions. There are the material flows, the information flows, and the cash flows. The entire logistics chain is dynamic and complicated. The core to understanding Practice competency is the ability to Define each value chain as they are presented. Every value chain is different and unique operationally. For the SCM leader to manage them, Define competency is needed to be able to allow the SCM leader to communicate, coordinate and collaborate well with people. Every defined practice begins with exploration and discovery. In Table 19, the Design Thinking Process starts with Empathy, and then Define. Empathy is about learning the customers' needs and pain points. Define is a discovery and divergent process to construct the customer's point of views and needs. As in the Ishikawa Chart or Fish-Bone Diagram, the fish head is the Problem defined by the team. The bones represent the various causes of the problems, typically, Man–Machine–Method–Materials–Management–Money. The Define element is a divergent process to unearth the causes of the problems, analyze, and synthesize to reach a defined problem statement. SCM leaders may use the brain-storming process and data collection to develop the Ishikawa Chart. Hence, some other literatures also call it the Cause-and-Effect diagram. Define competency helps the SCM leader to determine supply chain problems through the deployment of IoT, AT, and blockchain technologies throughout the supply chain. Hence, it is no more just a single ERP system or Office Automation application. It will be combining the best practices of technology knowhows to achieve SCM optimization. This is a key Practice competency in the SCM 3P Leadership Competency Framework.

Develop

The next Practice competency is Develop. Referring to Table 19 again, in the Design Thinking Process, there is the "prototyping" process in solutioning. Solutioning or solutions development is another key Practice competency for SCM leaders to acquire. With all the discovery and data collection, SCM leader needs to converge the thinking process through a convergent of ideation. With the problem statement established, SCM leaders can try out different routes and solutions to determine what the best option forward. This prototyping process certainly takes time and engagement to produce the desired outcome. In the SCM leaders' daily engagement, Develop competency helps them to engage with open-mindedness and develop supply chain solutions that are collaborative and produce win–win business partnerships.

Deliver

The third Practice competency is Deliver. The best way to understand the Deliver competency is the SCM leader's ability to deliver supply chain solutions to the customers to achieve the supply chain KPIs. The ability to solve customers' supply chain problems not only bring about customer satisfactions, it also brings about vibrant supply chain business to the organization concerned. Just as in the healthcare industry, it is all about Outcome! When the patient with certain illness goes to the hospital or consults the doctors, the patient is looking to a good outcome of healing. In the SCM, it is also all about the outcome. The supply chain KPIs are the measurements that will ensure the SCM leader's career longevity.

Recruiting New Supply Chain Talents

Most strong candidates for supply chain professionals these days examine the brand closely and also the leadership development strategies before coming on board. This applies to both entry-level and seasoned supply chain experts as indicated in my framework (Table 19). Here are some practices for attracting the brightest students and skilled professionals into your supply chain.

a. Use multichannel recruitment: The recruitment strategies of several companies quickly turn into "fill the hole for the moment" tasks. It is significant to be able to forecast supply and demand in logistics and SCM but it does not apply to the recruitment of supply chain talent well. Just a few companies have dedicated resources that concentrate on developing and managing supply chain talent pipelines and plans. The use of the multichannel approach goes ahead of the conventional one. The company can use tactics such as exhibiting at career fairs, post in social media and connecting with your website on career openings. It is not enough to have company sites with an "About" link together with a general "Jobs" one. Innovative organizations will use dedicated landing pages having direct links to the websites that are student-focused. Apart from positions and company information, the good sites give you case study profiles of successful professionals letting everyone know their experiences with the organization. Develop engaging and well-crafted stories about teams and individuals depicting them solving problems. Students always see conversations with the company representatives first at the time of the interview process. In this modern age of heavy social media and website use, the top organizations are adding new recruitment strategies that emphasize attractive supply chain careers instead of just posting the job requirements.
b. Tap on the value of councils and associations: Organizations that are recruiting a range of majors, must not overlook this extremely valuable resource. Advisory councils and boards of engineering and business colleges. Program advisory councils and boards together with the supply chain department are extremely useful. Associations such as APICS or CSCM in the United States are useful platforms to attract potential candidates globally.
c. Improve brand awareness for students and organizations: The established organizations operating in the business world have lit-

tle brand awareness among students. These companies need to work hard to aid the students to understand who they are and what they do. The company can also use recruitment agents to hire globally and advertise the supply chain opportunities the company is providing. Successful organizations measure brand awareness, provide info sessions, and pursue different speaking opportunities.

d. Tie up with alumni from top universities: The company needs to establish ties with various alumni as they have an abundance of volunteers and student leaders within them. The company will need innovative strategies for working with these student clubs such as having educational presentations at their chapter meetings and providing tours. Other things that are also of great value are their interactive programs that provide case-like challenges. This enables the organizations to evaluate the reactions of students to various challenging exercises.

Retaining Current Supply Chain Talents

Talent retention is one of the most essential facets of running a successful business. Although retaining talent in SCM is necessary to preserve a company's knowledge, high morale, satisfied customers, and even sales growth, retention strategies, and practices may be overlooked or unclear. The ability to maintain employees over time makes a huge impact on both sales and profits.

As the millennial generation has begun to dominate the workforce, turnover has increased and this group will make up 75% of the workforce. A recent study by Gallup group found that millennials have changed jobs three times as much in a year than their Baby Boomer counterparts. However, since the COVID-19 pandemic, there is an indication that this generation may now be intending to stay in their jobs for up to five years as opposed to two years as previously reported. The question is, how can you keep great talent from leaving every few years?

Leaders and managers want to understand their millennial talent in Asia but are missing the mark in their approach if sticking with what has been done in the past. People accepted a job and stuck with it largely due to receiving a paycheck and benefits previously. The status quo was just the way it was. Employees were satisfied with once-a-year reviews and salary increases. Or, maybe a team-building retreat and picnic were held occasionally to keep employees interested in staying with a job. Being unattached to a job was part and parcel of the working environment for many who would continue to stay.

These practices are no longer acceptable in today's workplace. Now, these supply chain talent chooses careers over a paycheck and wants a sense of purpose at work. The job and their life are closely integrated. Therefore, employees want to stay with a company that focuses on their development. Managers need to go beyond the role of being the "boss" and function more as coaches who develop strengths instead of concentrating just on weaknesses. SCM talent want ongoing conversations to stay engaged. There are three strategies we proposed to retain the existing supply chain talents.

Develop a Career Path for Each Employee

When recruiting, the message and branding from the company are very important. Conveying how the company values its employees and has structures in place for development should be part of your recruitment process. However, in retaining the talent, the walk has to match the talk. Providing opportunities to learn and grow are critical in retaining talent. Based on the proposed framework, we need a training plan to develop the existing staff to move from entry to expert level as shown in Table 20. In fact, the top five gaps in skills and competencies from the survey and interviews are the abilities to understand and deploy supply chain technologies. The gap is highest for artificial intelligence and machine learning, followed by supply chain automation, blockchain technology, and Industry 4.0 technologies. Thus, we need to provide trainings to narrow these gap and migrate these staff to become expert in their fields.

The amount of time spent training most operational roles is usually less than a month. However, large-scale training for this new employee base may be challenging and therefore needs to be planned appropri-

Table 20: Career path from entry to expert level

3Ps	Entry	Experienced	Expert
People	→	→	→

ately. In addition to traditional methods of training, other form of trainings may support bridging this gap.

i. Hands-on or on-the-job training: Leading by example is the backbone of leadership, and what could be better than learning on the job with the team?
ii. Technology-based learning: In the current world of COVID-19, technology could substitute in-person training with virtual training and simulation-based training.
iii. Peer-to-peer learning: Of the three prongs, "Peer-to-Peer Learning" is probably the best approach to scale. Training the trainer is a suitable way forward and provides a multiplier effect for training a large group. Not only does this method apply to managers and executives but also to hourly employees and workers.

Creating an environment that offers challenges and situations for development is imperative. Amazon recently announced that it will spend more than $700 million to train 100,000 employees for higher-skilled jobs. It's a six-year undertaking in which the company plans to reskill workers through its Amazon Technical Academy, Machine Learning University, Amazon Web Services Training and Certification program, and other programs. Workers are focused on improving their knowledge, skills, and career. Great talent wants to be rewarded with meaningful opportunities to advance. Retention practices must be put in place to address this need. Mentoring, coaching, and job shadowing are just a few that can be implemented.

Engage Fully with Each Employee

Employees want to feel connected to their work and they want to contribute. Their end goal is finding a good job that gives them a sense of purpose. By putting practices in place that stimulate engagement and give them compelling reasons to stay, the retention will increase. Having regular conversations with management is a solid way to engage employees.

Good talent wants to have ongoing communication with managers and others in order to feel valued. Setting up ways to give frequent feedback and provide opportunities for interactions increases employees' engagement. A core practice to put in place is scheduling regular one-on-one and small group meetings not only to check in on their projects but also to develop better relationships in learning what is important to them. Only then can the company create more opportunities that keep engagement high.

Offer Good Work–Life Balance

In today's workforce, the job role is just as important as the company and the value it places on its employees. Employees want to work for companies that invest in them both as employees and as people. SCM talent rate highly what a company can provide them in leading a better overall life. Almost 60% of millennials surveyed by Gallup said that work–life balance and personal well-being in a job are very important. As part of retention practices, companies need to implement programs to help employees reach their physical, community, social, and purpose goals. Putting practices in place for flexible work arrangements that may include flexible scheduling and work-from-home options can be great retention methods.

Appendix A

Survey Form in English

Dear Participant,

You are invited to participate in a research study titled "**Essential Skills for Supply Chain Professionals in Asia.**" This survey aims to understand the supply chain and logistics skills and competencies required for professionals in Asia, and suggest the key skills and knowledge areas that all professionals need to acquire to remain competitive in the future (next 5–10 years).

We highly value your participation in this study which will take not more than 10–12 minutes of your time. The survey is voluntary and strictly anonymous to maintain confidentiality and prevent the identification of specific respondents. Also, you can withdraw from the study at any time while completing the survey.

Thank you for your interest and participation in this study.

Dr. Albert Tan
albtan@mit.edu

STATEMENT BY PERSON AGREEING TO PARTICIPATE IN THIS STUDY

I have read and understood the information above and I freely and voluntarily give my consent to participate in this study.

○ Yes, I consent (1)
○ No, I do not consent (2)

Skip To: End of Survey If Dear Participant, you are invited to participate in a research study titled "Seven Traits for... = No, I do not consent

Q1 How many years of experience do you have as a supply chain/logistics professional?

- ○ 0–2 Years (1)
- ○ 3–5 Years (2)
- ○ 6–10 Years (3)
- ○ 10–15 Years (9)
- ○ 15–25 Years (10)
- ○ Above 25 Years (11)
- ○ I am not a supply chain/logistics professional (12)

Skip To: End of Survey If How many years of experience you have as a supply chain/logistics professional? = I am not a supply chain/logistics professional

Q2 Your Gender

- ○ Male (1)
- ○ Female (2)

Q3 Your Age

- ○ 18–24 (1)
- ○ 25–34 (4)
- ○ 35–44 (5)
- ○ 45–55 (6)
- ○ Above 55 (7)

Q4 Your Nationality

▼ Afghanistan (1) ... Zimbabwe (1357)

Q5 Please mention your country of residence (where you live and work)

▼ Afghanistan (1) ... Zimbabwe (1357)

Q6 Please mention your role/position level in the organization
○ Entry/junior level (1)
○ Mid level (2)
○ Senior level (3)
○ Top management/leadership team (4)
○ Others (Please specify) (5) ________________

Q7 Your educational level
○ High school/diploma (1)
○ Bachelor's degree (4)
○ Master's degree or above (5)
○ Others (Please specify) (6) ________________

Q8 Please select your organization type from the below category
○ Private sector firm (subsidiary of a foreign/multinational firm) (5)
○ Private sector firm (local/home-grown) (1)
○ Private sector firm (joint-venture between foreign and local firm) (6)
○ Semi-government firm (3)
○ Public sector firm (4)
○ Other (Please specify) (2) ________________

Q9 Which of the following industry/sector most closely matches the one in which you are employed?
○ Tourism and hospitality (1)
○ Construction and real estate (2)
○ Educational services (3)
○ Airline/aviation (4)
○ Manufacturing (5)
○ Retail and trading (6)
○ Healthcare (7)
○ Transportation, logistics, and supply chain (8)
○ Public administration/services (16)

- O Banking and finance (9)
- O Information technology (IT) (10)
- O Media, entertainment, and recreation (13)
- O Food and agriculture (21)
- O Others (Please specify) (17) ________________________

Q10 How many employees are working in your organization?

- O 1–9 (1)
- O 10–49 (2)
- O 50–99 (3)
- O 100–249 (4)
- O 250–499 (5)
- O 500–999 (8)
- O 1000 or more (9)

Q11 How long you have been working in the present organization?

- O Less than 3 months (1)
- O 3–6 months (2)
- O 7–12 months (3)
- O 1–3 years (4)
- O 4–5 years (5)
- O 6–10 years (6)
- O Greater than 10 years (7)

Q12 Please rate the importance of the following skills and competencies for you would require as a supply chain professional to be competitive (1) At Present and (2) In the Future (Next 5–10 Years) on a Scale of 1–5 (1—Not all Important; 2—Slightly Important; 3—Moderately Important; 4—Very Important, and 5—Extremely Important). Please enter the response as a numeric value.

	Present	Future
	(1–5) (1)	(1–5) (1)
Awareness of mobile technologies (12)		
Information technology skill (52)		

(*Continued*)

	Present		Future	
	(1–5)	(1)	(1–5)	(1)
Integration of information flow and systems externally (53)				
Integration of information flow and systems internally (54)				
Knowledge of the latest technology (55)				
Software knowledge (56)				
Spreadsheet abilities (57)				
Demand forecasting (58)				
Distribution planning (59)				
Facilities location (60)				
Inventory management (61)				
Knowledge of the logistics or manufacturing industry (62)				
Materials handling (63)				
Order processing (64)				
Purchasing (65)				
Return goods handling (66)				
Reverse supply chain (67)				
Salvage and scrap disposal (68)				
Supply chain costing skill (69)				
Supply chain-oriented knowledge (70)				
Transport management (71)				
Transportation regulation (72)				
Warehousing management (73)				
Ability to prioritize (74)				
Ability to see the "Big Picture" (75)				
Benchmarking ability (76)				
Change management (77)				
Conflict management (78)				
Cross-functional coordination skill (79)				
ISO 14000 Standards (80)				
Knowledge of cultural differences (81)				

(*Continued*)

(*Continued*)

	Present	Future
	(1–5) (1)	(1–5) (1)
Knowledge of environmental issues (82)		
Leadership skill (83)		
Negotiation skill (84)		
Oral communication (85)		
People skill (86)		
Project management (87)		
Quality management (88)		
Quantitative modeling skill (89)		
Statistical analysis (90)		
Team orientation (91)		
Written communication (92)		

Q13 Would like to share three essential competencies that have enabled you to become a competent logistics or supply chain professional? Please give example for each competency in your work.

Competency 1: ____

____

Competency 2: ____

____

Competency 3: ____

____

Appendix B

Survey Form in Chinese

亚洲供应链经理能力

亲爱的参与者，

您受邀参与一项题为“亚洲供应链经理的七项能力”的研究。本次调查旨在了解亚洲管理人员在内保持竞争力所需的本调查旨在了解未来5年亚洲的供应链和物流管理人员所需的技能和能力我们很高兴您参与本次研究，这份问卷将占用您不超过10-12分钟的时间。调查是自愿匿名参与。此外，您可以在完成调查问卷期间随时退出。感谢您对本研究的参与。

同意参与本研究的个人声明

我已阅读并理解上述信息，并同意参与本研究。

- 是的，我同意
- 不，我不同意

您作为供应链/物流专业人士有多少年的经验？

○ 0–2 年
○ 3–5 年
○ 6–10 年
○ 10–15 年
○ 15–25 年
○ 25 年以上
○ 我不是供应链/物流专业人士

- -

您的性别

○ 男
○ 女

- -

你的年龄

○ 18–24
○ 25–34
○ 35–44
○ 45–55
○ 55 以上

- -

你的国籍 ____

- -

请选择您的居住国家（您居住和工作的地方）

____

请选择您在组织中的角色/职位级别
○ 入门/初级
○ 中级
○ 高级
○ 最高管理层/领导团队
○ 其他（请注明）＿＿＿＿＿＿＿＿＿＿＿＿＿＿＿

你的教育水平
○ 高中
○ 学士学位
○ 硕士及以上
○ 其他（请注明）＿＿＿＿＿＿＿＿＿＿＿＿＿＿＿

请从以下类别中选择您的组织类型
○ 私营部门公司（外国/跨国公司的子公司）
○ 私营部门公司（本地公司）
○ 私营部门公司（合资企业）
○ 半国营公司
○ 全资国营公司
○ 其他（请注明）＿＿＿＿＿＿＿＿＿＿＿＿＿＿＿

以下哪个行业/部门与您受雇的行业/部门最匹配？
○ 旅游和酒店服务
○ 建筑和房地产
○ 教育服务
○ 航空业
○ 制造
○ 零售和贸易

- ○ 医疗保健
- ○ 运输、物流和供应链
- ○ 公共行政/服务
- ○ 银行和金融
- ○ 信息技术 (IT)
- ○ 媒体、娱乐和休闲
- ○ 食品和农业
- ○ 其他（请注明）______________________________

您的组织有多少员工？

- ○ 1–9
- ○ 10–49
- ○ 50–99
- ○ 100–249
- ○ 250–499
- ○ 500–999
- ○ 1000 及以上

你在现在的组织工作多久了

- ○ 少于3月
- ○ 3–6月
- ○ 7–12月
- ○ 1–3 年
- ○ 4–5 年
- ○ 6–10 年
- ○ 大于 10 年

作为供应链专业人士，你需要在未来5年内具备的竞争力，请按照1-5分(1 -不是所有的重要;2 -稍微重要;中度重要;4-非常重要5 -非常重要)将以下技能和能力的“重要性”进行评分。

	未来的重要性 请输入数值1-5之间	现在的重要性 请输入数值1-5之间
供应链能力		
分销规划和管理		
需求预测		
设施位置规划/选择		
仓库管理		
资产和库存管理		
供应链流程化/整合(内部和外部)		
供应链政策、法律法规		
战略采购/采购		
供应链流程再造/优化		
运输/车队管理		
逆向物流		
供应链成本和预算		
第三方物流管理		
关系管理(客户、供应商、海关等)		
货运管理		
生产计划与调度		
定量建模技巧		
IT能力		
区块链设计开发		
供应链分析		
电子商务技术		
电子采购		
供应链自动化		
工业4.0技术行业		
软件编程		
人工智能和机器学习		
ERP实施		

	未来的重要性 请输入数值1-5之间	现在的重要性 请输入数值1-5之间
仓库管理软件		
运输管理软件		
软件设计		
管理能力		
循环经济		
ISO 14000标准		
精益工具和方法		
起草合同		
六西格玛方法和实施		
决策技巧		
标杆管理技能		
跨部门协调能力		
风险管理		
团队定位		
变更管理		
冲突管理		
跨文化管理		
质量管理		
项目管理		
时间管理		
领导能力		
谈判技巧		
软技能		

您能否分享一个案例，通过特定知识或能力帮助您成为物流或供应链专业人士的例子?

____
____
____
____
____

如果您希望收到这项研究的简报，请提供您的详细信息(可选)
姓名 ____
邮箱____

Appendix C

List of Companies Interviewed

A.P. Moller MaerskVietnam Ltd. is the first 100% foreign-owned company within the Vietnam logistics industry. Since 1991, Maersk Vietnam Ltd. has represented Maersk and Sealand. The company's head office is located in Ho Chi Minh City, employing more than 1,600 people with 11 offices across Vietnam, Cambodia and Myanmar, and Laos. With 30 years of local market experience, the Maersk team is uniquely placed to help connect customers to Asia and the rest of the world through seamless connections to our extensive Intra-Asia and Global service network.

Cargill Vietnam works alongside farmers, producers, manufacturers, retailers, governments, and other organizations to fulfill the purpose to nourish the world in a safe, responsible, and sustainable way.

Central Retail in Vietnam was established in 2012 with only Fashion business. Throughout its nine-year operation in Vietnam, Central Retail continues to develop and transform Vietnam's modern trade and retail sector. Today, the company proudly welcomes an average of 175,000 customers every day at more than 280 malls & stores across 39 provinces nationwide in a total retail area of more than 1,000,000 square meters, provides employment and career opportunities for nearly 15,000 employees in Vietnam. Central Retail's three key growth drivers including Food, Non-Food and Property provide customers with a diverse portfolio of retail brands, including GO! Mall, GO! Hypermarket, Tops Market, Big C, go!, Lan Chi Mart, Nguyen Kim, Supersports, LookKool, Kubo, Hello Beauty, and Robins.

Chilibeli.com is an online shopping application for daily products such as fruit, vegetables, basic necessities, and other household needs that carries the concept of social commerce — buying and selling activities that involve social interaction between users in a community through online and offline social networks. Products from farmers and producers of FMCG (Fast Moving Customer Goods) will be connected directly to Chilibeli Partners, whose role is to make it easier for people around them to shop easily to get quality fresh products in an environment. being able to make it easier for people in the surrounding environment, Chilibeli Partners can get extra income or additional spending money from every transaction for each member of their community, with the flexibility to manage time for other things.

Mega Group is an Indian Conglomerate, founded by Kishore Biyani and HQ in Mumbai, India. Set up in 2013 it has national brand Big Bazar (floor space approx. 30,000 sq. feet) as part of Future Retail and employs about 50,000 people. The Group has faced severe challenges to its retail business due to the pandemic leading to losses in bottom line. Besides its attempt to shift to eCommerce in a big way, Mega Group, with the large format Big Bazar has entered in small format (500–3000 sq. feet) business with four brands Nilgiris, Easy Day (earlier Bharti-Walmart), Heritage-food supply chain. Mega Group is being supported by Reliance vendors; their SAP is used for planning by Mega Group.

Giant Distribution Centre established in Malaysia by the early 1970s is the largest food retailer in Malaysia categorized in terms of sales and the number of retail outlets The retailer operates hypermarkets and supermarkets nationwide under the different brands. The brand of supermarkets and hypermarkets is well known as a home-grown trusted brand in Malaysia. The brand is well-known to local shoppers as a retailer that offers the best value-for-money for the products purchased by consumers. The brands targets the mass market and classified as the largest supermarket chain in Malaysia.

Green Renewable Organic World Centre Sdn Bhd specializes in sustainability and waste management projects, sustainable farm systems, aquaculture, and microalgae production, use of agriculture biomass for biofuels, biofertilizer and bioproducts, development of organic/natural farms, cultural, rural eco-agro tourism enterprises; remote sensing applications in precision agriculture utilizing AI-empowered satellite & UAV platforms.

GS1 Malaysia Berhad is a member of GS1, a non-profit global supply chain standards organization, dedicated to the design and implementation of global solutions and standards to improve the efficiency and visibility of supply chains in all sectors worldwide. The GS1 System was introduced in Malaysia in July 1988. In Malaysia, GS1 Malaysia Berhad is the only official source for GS1 barcode numbers and standards. GS1 Malaysia Berhad enables its more than 6,000 members of all sizes from over 10 sectors across Malaysia to enhance their efficiency and cost effectiveness by adopting GS1 global supply chain best practices.

PKT Logistics Group Sdn Bhd is a socially responsible company providing logistics services by utilizing local human resources, building environmentally friendly warehouses, open engagement with the communities, inspire other businesses to provide positive impact to people and communities through its activities. Among the industry verticals ventured by our group includes automotive logistics, FMCG logistics, F&B logistics, electronic & electrical logistics, frozen & chill logistics, e-commerce logistics, and port logistics.

Procter & Gamble Vietnam is a subsidiary of Procter & Gamble (P&G), an American multinational corporation with one of the strongest portfolios of trusted, quality, leadership brands. P&G Vietnam was one of the first American companies to invest in Vietnam after the normalization of the diplomatic relations between Vietnam and the United States in 1995 and has achieved double-digit growth for many years and has grown 12 times larger for the last ten years. With the commitment to "Touching and improving more Vietnamese consumers' lives," for the past 25 years, P&G Vietnam serves Vietnamese consumers through a portfolio of leadership brands across a wide range of consumer product categories, including Baby Care, Hair Care, Fabric & Home Care, Grooming, Skin & Personal Care,

Feminine Care, and Oral Care. The company operates two large-scale manufacturing facilities in Binh Duong province in addition to a general office in HCMC.

Siam Cement Group Logistics is a subsidiary company under Siam Cement Group (SCG), the biggest Cement-building materials, chemicals, and packaging business in Thailand. SCG Logistics services cover inland, multimodal transport, warehousing, and fulfillment for B2B, C2C, and E-commerce sector. The company's vision is to become the most dominant 3PL with the strongest and largest network coverage in Thailand.

Sitics Logistic Solutions Pvt. Ltd. was founded by A.M.Sikander and Haridas.T. The company was registered in 2007 with a vision of providing services with the highest ethical values to customers and employees. The company evolved into a full-fledged logistics organization as the founders were providing services to a few corporates including MNCs and saw the huge potential of Logistics as a service, as there was a dearth of quality services being offered. The market was vast and services offered were inadequate and fragmented. Sitics grew from existing clientele who offered more business and the reputation of the company grew through word of mouth as a reliable partner who can be trusted with large contracts in multiple sites. From being a small organization, the company quickly grew into a mid-size company as new customers were added and current customers entrusted them with more business.

SNT Global Logistics offer both B2B & B2C logistics solutions for fast-moving consumer goods (FMCG), retail, eCommerce, consumer electronics, fashion, cosmetics, and skincare companies. With a total of 8 warehouses across Malaysia and Singapore, SNT Global has been growing at a rapid pace and plans to expand their business in Asia in the future with their partners. The company has recently **expanded** their e-commerce services by providing global tracking capabilities for the clients.

Sri Trang Gloves (Thailand) Public Company is a manufacturing and distributor of high-quality natural latex and nitrile examination gloves in Thailand.

Tiki (abbr. for "Tìm kiếm & Tiết kiệm," which means "Search & Save") is the fastest and most trusted B2C E-commerce platform in Vietnam. Tiki is well-known for its unique TikiNow service (2-Hour Delivery), world-class customer service with a 80+ NPS score, and diverse categories of 100% authentic products. Tiki is an all-in-one commercial ecosystem, consisting of member companies such as:

- Tiki Trading and Exchange offer 10 million products from 26 categories serving millions of customers nationwide.
- Tikinow Smart Logistics Co., Ltd ("TNSL") is a provider of end-to-end logistics services, transportation services, postal services for E-commerce platform www.tiki.vn
- Ti Ki Joint Stock Company ("TiKi") is the unit that establishes and organizes the e-commerce platform www.tiki.vn so that sellers can conduct part or the whole process of buying and selling goods, services on the e-commerce platform.
- Ti Ki Trading Company Limited ("Tiki Trading") is a unit that sells goods and services on the e-commerce platform.

Unilever Thai Trading Ltd. is a wholly owned subsidiary of Unilever, the Anglo-Dutch multinational. Unilever is one of the largest fast-moving consumer goods manufacturers in Thailand. The company was first established in Thailand in 1932 as Siam Industries (1932) Ltd., manufacturing soaps, candles, and edible oils and fats. The company was renamed Lever Brothers (Thailand) Ltd. in 1954 and then Unilever Thai Holdings Ltd. in September 1997. The Home and Personal Care/Ice Cream factory is at Ladkrabang where a wide range of consumer products are manufactured. The foods factory (Gateway) is located Southeast of Bangkok. Operations of Unilever in Thailand are split into Unilever Thai Holdings Ltd, and Unilever Thai Trading Ltd. In 2010, the company declared "Sustainable Living Plan" which is one of the most challenging purposes for world and resource sustainability. Unilever has targeted that the company will improve the quality of life, health, and living of more than 1 billion consumers within year 2020. And also, the company intends to obtain all materials from the farm that has no impact on environment, and it will reduce half of the environmental impact from its operations and products, in addition to reduce half of the using of Unilever's products.

Zespri was formed as a co-operative of kiwifruit growers in New Zealand in 1997. Its international headquarters are in Mount Maunganui, New Zealand. Zespri portfolio of kiwifruit varieties includes SunGold, Green, and Organic. With sales revenues of $3.1 billion, the Zespri™ Brand is recognized as the world leader in premium-quality kiwifruit. Based in New Zealand, we are 100 percent owned by current or past kiwifruit growers, and employ approximately 550 people globally. Zespri's top competitors include Canada Bread, FreshPoint, Bob's Red Mill, and Chiquita Brands. Zespri is a company that manufactures and supplies food products.

Zimmer India (zimmerindia.com) is a US company in personalized joint replacement in the healthcare industry. The company imports into India joints from its manufacturing facilities in the UK. Since the business involves very specialized logistics where market trends of items to be kept in stock and nature of demand of different joints needs in-depth knowledge of nature of demand for different hospitals specialied in joint replacement as also preference of different doctors for brands like Zimmer, J&J etc, customer-related in-depth information and knowledge is a valuable input into inventory management and logistics. The supply lead time for these items can be anything from 6 to 24 months and therefore needs internal review of inventory every 45 days also. New design of joints are added very slowly as average life of a design can be anything up to 12 years.

Appendix D: Additional Interviews from Companies

Interview from China

oTMS

Company Overview

Created in 2011, oTMS is China's leading transport management platform that connects shippers, 3PLs, carriers, drivers, and consignees on a single workflow. Mr Mirek is the CEO of oTMS in China. The concept was first designed to solve the major problems of transport industry that inherently relies on multitier outsourcing. Today, oTMS provides oneTMS — cloud transport management system and Orange — comprehensive transport outsourcing service including 4PL and optimization consulting.

oTMS end-2-end carrier management including carrier sourcing, procurement, dynamic allocation, daily execution, real-time visibility via apps, IoT and API performance monitoring, billing, payment, and data analysis. oTMS helps customers to increase transport visibility of shipments, carrier service levels, and reduce cost in a sustainable way.

We currently employ approximately 70 people in Shanghai, Beijing, and Guangzhou. About 15 could be considered "supply chain staff" involved in transport control tower/4PL services.

What are the key goals and targets that you have set for your supply chain staff?

This depends on the function within 4PL unit, main goals are:

- o Procurement and Logistics (P&L) revenue, gross margin, and net contribution for department head

- o New revenue and gross margin for sales & solutions staff
- o Various operation key performance indicators include on time delivery, customer satisfaction for operational staffs

What are the essential skills or competencies for decision-making for supply chain issues?

- o TMS is position in a unique position in China's logistics services sector, using modern technology and process-oriented approach to service level and cost improvement of legacy supply chains, helping customers to transform their legacy workflows. We pioneer this approach here. Moreover, we operate at intersection of physical logistics services, dealing with shippers' supply chain and procurement departments and software, dealing with information technology (IT) organizations. Our projects are complex not just technically but also organizationally.

  Finding right people and identifying right competency skillset is a challenge, except for fundamental skills of a given role (say operation experience in a 3PL for ops team member of our 4PL team, or sales experience in a software or 3PL vendor) we struggle to find people who:
- o Worked in reputable MNCs early in their careers where they were encouraged to learn independently and take initiative, had proven career progression record
- o Have experience in enterprise system implementations and process transformation, are enthusiastic about digitization potential and exhibit clear buy-in of our mission and solution portfolio during the interviews
- o Sufficiently detail-oriented to be able to guide the customer through the implementation/transformation phase from the role of the trusted expert, with sufficient communication and interpersonal skills
- o Have proven project management skills, including PMP certification for specific roles

- o Exhibit further growth potential and interest in parallel moves such as from 4PL to software services and vice versa (obviously that excludes technical roles like software developers)

Where do you see yourself in the next 5 years?

We plan to expand out oTMS overseas along with planned/in progress APAC expansion assuming COVID-19 is over.

Is there anything that you would like to add to be a competent supply chain manager?

Having years of vertical experience and ability to run routine department operations is not going to be enough in fast-changing business environment in China. I feel, after 20 years here in different roles, the biggest obstacle in China is too hierarchical mindset where people are not expected to challenge their bosses and peers and do not come up with own initiative but rely on top-down direction. In case of supply chain management (SCM) department the thing is that any transformation is rarely going to come from the very top. SCM manager should value more critical thinking and initiative in their own teams, allocate more resources away from routine tasks to learn and explore what other companies are doing including digitization.

Interview from Brunei

Gong Cha

Company Overview

Gong Cha is a global bubble tea franchise that began in Kaohsiung, Taiwan in 2006. Historically, the ancient art of serving tea to royalty, such as the Emperor of China, is known as "Gong Cha." Similarly, Gong Cha aspires to deliver only the highest-quality tea to everyone by offering natural, nutritious, freshly brewed tea, and refreshing beverages. Last year, Gong Cha Korea was at the vanguard of that global expansion, with 777 outlets open by the end of 2021. Korea is the world's largest Gong Cha market, and the country is at the forefront of the brand's innovation and international expansion. Its brand has spread throughout Brunei's neighbors, including Malaysia, Singapore, Hong Kong, China, Macau, the Philippines, and others. Gong Cha is currently the fastest-growing brand in the world, with over 1,700 outlets in South Korea, Japan, the United States, Canada, and other countries. During the epidemic last year, Gong Cha significantly increased its footprint in several key regions, including Australia, Japan, the Philippines, New York, and Mexico. This achievement, however, would not have been possible without the unwavering support and dedication of the company people, suppliers, franchise partners, and, ultimately, the valued consumers. People are at the center of Gong Cha, and we establish and uphold the highest standards when it comes to doing the right thing for our people. Gong Cha conducts business and builds relationships based on the fundamental principles of integrity, innovation, pragmatic, and inspiration.

What are the key goals and targets that you have set for your supply chain staff?

The Gong Cha supply chain is a profit center, with procurement functions divided into drink ingredients, consumables, and bar/kitchen equipment. For the support centers and directly owned locations, Gong Cha also purchases fixtures, fittings, and furniture, as well as IT and office supplies. Other services are purchased on a case-by-case basis. Gong Cha Global Ltd.-related organizations have over 150 vendors, encompassing products such as tea, pearls, toppings equipment, and other services. Thus, Gong Cha is devoted to providing on-time service with a rapid and seamless operation. COVID-19 has made online food and beverage (F&B) delivery a general trend toward e-commerce, rising urbanization, and shifting social patterns. Similarly, Gong Cha delivery services are committed to ensuring their people are able to adapt to the social distancing procedures that were necessary to prevent the virus from spreading. It is important to ensure the delivery services able to efficiently and safely reach out to intended customers.

According to Mr Nicky, the Master Franchisor at Gong Cha Brunei, his team are committed to delivering rapid and seamless operations toward reducing the overall operation costs. He added, his company is looking forward to technology adoption including artificial intelligence (AI), which may assist in improving day-to-day business operation and at the same time may reduce manpower. With the technology adoption, the company may improve the product quality, affordability, keeping the food fresh, and increase productivity. In addition, the adoption of technology can aid in the elimination of safety concerns. Technology allows more complex jobs to be completed 24 hours a day, 7 days a week, and able to reduce the number of workplace injuries.

With the new norm, effective and efficient delivery services are so crucial as they may provide high levels of accessibility to customers. Delivery services are willing to deliver things of various types and sizes to customers without compromising on quality. Alike, effective and efficient delivery services are required in order to satisfy the demands and provide a convenient customer experience in the COVID-19 situation. Contactless delivery service has also become a norm in which food is left at clients' doors, and payments are made online. Hence, technology adoption plays an important role to ensure the entire Gong Cha delivery services are smooth. At Gong Cha, it is hoped that the adoption of technology should simplify the entire business operations that will bring high-level customer satisfaction.

What are the essential skills or competencies for decision-making for supply chain issues?

One of the most important skills that Mr Nicky highlighted is time management skills. Time management skills are in high demand, just like other soft skills including organizing skills. Employers will evaluate employee time management skills as well as the efficacy of the overall team in achieving organizational goals. Effective time management necessitates employees analyzing their workload, assigning priorities, and maintaining a laser-like concentration on productive tasks. Employees who are good in time management can avoid distractions and engage the help among coworkers to achieve organization objectives. Some of the top time management skills that need to take into day-to-day operation are to first know to prioritize the assigned task. It may be impossible to do every single minute duty that has been assigned, thus, should be prioritized so that the most critical things in a logical manner can be done. Second, scheduling is essential. Scheduling has an impact on daily, weekly, and monthly tasks as well as the workflow of others. Schedules can also help prevent procrastinating. Third, keeping a to-do list is an excellent technique to avoid forgetting crucial tasks. It takes energy to remember all assigned tasks, can be exhausting and daunting to think about everything that needs to complete all week, thus dividing all of the necessary jobs into daily lists will be the best solution. Next, workload management will assist the employee to know and enforce the ideal workload that may improve stability in work performance and prevents burnout. Hence, it is critical to resist the urge to overwork. It is important to include required breaks and a reasonable time to end the workday in the day-to-day schedule. Lastly, work delegation is necessary. Employees should be able to delegate some responsibilities depending on the type of work being assigned. Knowing what to delegate and when to delegate is a crucial skill. Both techniques will improve productivity and reduce costs in the long run if they can be managed well.

In addition, Mr Nicky enhanced the need for leadership skills. As a leader, communication skill is essential, covering everything from organizational goals to specific assignments to staff in a clear and concise manner. Leaders must be able to communicate effectively in a variety of settings, including one-on-one, departmental, and full-staff talks, as well as communication by phone, email, video, chat, and social media. In addition, leaders must also always motivate staff to go above and beyond organization expectations. Motivation may include building employee self-esteem through recognition and prizes and assigning new duties to boost employee interest in the organization. Moreover, a pleasant leader's attitude or positivity may go a long way. For instance, when things don't go as planned, a good leader should be able to promote a joyful and healthy work environment, even during hectic, stressful times. Employees who feel they work in a favorable environment are more likely to result in more productivity and are more willing to work long hours when necessary. Alike, a good leader must also be always creative. Leaders must make a number of judgments for which there is no clear answer. Most of the employees will be amazed and inspired by a leader who does not always take the easy way out. Some of the qualities associated with creative thinking include sound judgment, innovation, and embracing diverse cultural perspectives. Comparable, leaders should always encourage and give full support to employees to provide meaningful information on their performance. However, leaders should draw a line to avoid micromanaging them. Employees will also admire a leader who always gives straightforward yet compassionate feedback.

Furthermore, Mr Nicky also strengthens the importance of technology skills. With various technology arriving in the next few years, these skills will help to improve overall operations which will result in more productive and efficient day-to-day operation, hence directly affecting the organization's goals and targets. Employees will gain more confidence in using developing technologies and will be able to complete tasks more quickly if able to develop these skills. Having technology skills, for example, will assist an organization to save money and time by allowing internal employees to fix a technological problem on their own. Constantly updating technology skills will aid to complete tasks more quickly, prevents future technological issues by allowing for greater collaboration, versatility, and improve security in the organization.

Is there anything that you would like to add to be a competent supply chain manager?

Brunei's economy, which is quickly rising on a national and international scale, relies heavily on the F&B business. Higher domestic demand as a result of the COVID-19 outbreak has boosted sales of online F&B. The value of F&B services sales was anticipated to be BND84.9 million. Thus, in the face of tough competition and swiftly shifting trends, it might be difficult to maintain F&B sales without the right skills. Finding a balance between getting new customers and retaining existing customers is crucial to success. Creating a strategy and breaking it down into doable steps is the best way to tackle any new goal. Thus, business intelligence skills, insights, and overall data organization and utilization skills will continue to be major priorities in managing the supply chain network. Supply chain issues are multilayered and ongoing, and a lack of supply chain integration might jeopardize the entire business operations. Alike, soft and hard skills are also important in order to stay competitive with economic demands in an increasingly competitive environment while also preparing a future workforce.

Interview from Bangladesh

Interport Group

Company Overview

The Interport Group from Bangladesh is a significant provider and is well known for its maritime services. It was formed in 2001 by Mr Mohiuddin Abdul Kadir (also known as Capt. MAK), a renowned marine expert and leader with over 40 years of experience who has made important contributions to Bangladesh's maritime and logistics sectors. Interport Group developed its service offerings and diversified into additional fields under the strategic guidance of the Company's Board and Management, from Marine Survey to Freight Forwarding, Liner Shipping Agency, Contract and Off-Shore Logistics, Corporate Training, and Consultancy. Mr Mohiuddin thereafter enrolled as an Advocate of the Supreme Court of Bangladesh and began a career in Admiralty and Maritime Law before handing over the family firm to his capable successors. Mr Mohiuddin began bringing the next generation into the family firm and entrusting them with management duties. Engr. Tanjil Ahmed Ruhullah currently serves as Managing Director for the Group, while Mrs Razia Sultana and Mr Taasin Ahmed Asadullah serve as Chairperson and Director, respectively. According to Mr Mohiuddin, the company's largest assets are its people, as expressed in their group's motto "Powered by people, driven by values." The management believes that they are able to exceed clients' expectations every day by adhering to the fundamental values of teamwork, quality, and integrity. Interport exists to deliver the finest possible services in Bangladeshi ports to its customers, whether they are ship owners, ship managers, or charterers. Interport works carefully and responsibly with its customers to guarantee that they meet and surpass short-term profit targets while achieving long-term strategic market goals. In addition, Interport promotes its clients' services aggressively in order to maximize income and cut expenses by shortening ship and container turnaround times in Bangladeshi ports. To achieve the intended results, Interport is devoted to fostering cutting-edge business procedures that combine technology with Interport employees' talents and experience. The company is focused on its customers' needs and operates flexibly, acknowledging that shipping is a capital-intensive business with different priorities and objectives for each primary.

What are the key goals and targets that you have set for your supply chain staff?

With the company vision to make Bangladesh's maritime industry a global leader in terms of openness, integrity, efficiency, and professionalism, Interport Group is continuously improved their supply chain through greater consistency in the quality of maritime and logistics service offered. It is coupled with the need to squeeze costs out of the supply chain network, through greater control. However, professionalism is the main concern that all employees at Interport Group should exhibit. It means that one entity should treat the other with the same level of respect and trust, and should not intervene or command the other in any way. All parties engaged should securely safeguard classified information. All parties should be required to follow the terms and conditions set out. This is the main core at Interport Group to ensure all stakeholders are equally treated and get the best services that they required. Alike, Interport Group is endlessly building leadership across the seven seas (Character, Competence, Courage, Commitment, Caring, Communicating, and Community) to promote fairness and justice within the business and in society at large.

The interview that took place on March 22, 2022 with logistics experts, Mr Mohammad Nazmuzzaman Hye, the General Manager of logistics and supply chain at Interport Group, emphasized a few areas that are critical to remain competitive. To ensure that the company's main goal can be achieved particularly fluctuating customer demand, it is important to improve customer value and be more responsive to address any customer enquiries, thus, leas to customer loyalty. Alike, it is also important to build a good network among all the stakeholders as a strategy to generate current and future company income. Thus, it is imperative to be efficient in managing the entire supply chain network. It cannot be done without great teamwork because collaborative problem-solving produces better results. People who have the backing of a team are more inclined to take calculated risks that lead to creativity. Working in a group fosters personal development, boosts job satisfaction, and reduces stress. In the end, it enables to accelerate company cash flow.

What are the essential skills or competencies for decision-making for supply chain issues?

In addition, according to Mr Mohammad, communication skills, networking skills, planning skills, negotiation skill, and problem-solving skills is the five essential skills and competencies for staff in meeting the company goals and targets. First, to allow others and oneself to absorb information more properly and rapidly, good communication skills are required. Poor communication skills, however, lead to a lot of misunderstanding and frustration that will jeopardize the entire supply chain operations. Thus, the staff needs to use, improve, and show great communication skills that will help advance in the profession while also making more competitive, particularly in winning customer heart. For instance, active listening enables staff to get respect from not only coworkers but from all the stakeholders. It may also improve workplace understanding. Similarly, knowing how to communicate effectively is a crucial talent. Information can be delivered more effectively when someone is able to communicate more effectively. Furthermore, friendly characteristics such as honesty and friendliness can aid in the development of trust and understanding when interacting at work. Confident communication is beneficial not only in the workplace but also increases the likelihood that people will respond positively to ideas offered with confidence. Thus, communication skills are the main important skills that the majority of the supply chain staff should have.

Alike, having excellent networking skills is required to build a supply chain resilient. It is part of communication, active listening, and social skills that are incredibly essential in both professional and personal settings. It is the skill that is especially sought after by most employers including at the Interport Group. Successful firms rely heavily on networking. Networking skills are the abilities required to maintain professional and social relationships. Networking is an important skill in sales, corporate growth, and a variety of other fields, particularly in the maritime and logistics industry. To build and cultivate relationships with new contacts and promote something of organizational value, networking abilities are required. In addition, planning skills are another important attribute that the company are looking at according to Mr Mohammad. In the context of the supply chain, planning skills are referred to as the forward-looking process of organizing assets to maximize the flow of goods, services, and information from a supplier to a customer while balancing supply and demand. Demand planning, inventory planning, production planning and scheduling, distribution planning, sales and operations planning, and a few others are examples of planning skills.

Moving forward, negotiation skill is the abilities that affect not only the outcome of individual deals but also supplier relationships and overall success. Negotiating often involves the cost of an item, delivery time, and quality requirements in the supply chain context. The perfect negotiation culminates in a win–win outcome. Accordingly, all sides must begin negotiations with a clear purpose in mind. Lastly, supply chain managers nowadays will employ a combination of tools, strategies, and approaches to meet daily and long-term difficulties as multinational supply chains become more complicated. Thus, problem-solving skills or decision-making skills are of the utmost importance. Problem-solving is also an organized way to deal with a problem that can lead to the best solution. When done effectively, it can provide someone with a sense of control and predictability when dealing with an issue. Thus, it's critical that the supply chain leader is able to recognize the problem, define and analyze it, produce alternative solutions, locate solutions for specific areas of the problem, propose a decision-making process, implement the solution, and assess its success.

Accordingly, Mr Mohammad also specified that, in addition to the aforementioned skills, well-rounded education in supply chain and logistics management is critical for the long-term success of the organization and the supply chain profession's survival. There are many innovative approaches to increase supply chain professionals' skills and keep them current on the latest supply chain competencies. Hence, always be adaptable and refer to the right people to excel in new responsibilities.

Major Skill Sets Required Before, During, and After the COVID-19 Pandemic

The COVID-19 pandemic has forced employees to adjust their work habits almost immediately. The COVID-19 pandemic has heightened the urgency of this quick change. Individuals in all industries must learn to adapt to quickly changing circumstances, and businesses must learn how to match those workers to new roles and activities. This dynamic encompasses more than remote working or the role of automation and AI. It's about how leaders may reskill and upskill their employees in the post-pandemic environment to deliver new business models. Hence, companies should design a talent strategy that improves employees' digital and cognitive skills, as well as their social and emotional skills, adaptability, and resilience, to face this challenge. Now is the time for businesses to commit to reskilling by increasing their learning spending. Companies will be better prepared for future upheavals if they develop this muscle.

According to Mr Mohammad, today's supply chain managers must be aware of more than simply their own company's activities. They must also be aware of what is happening around the world. Maintaining some industry awareness and being informed of current supply chain developments are desirable attributes in a potential employee. Thus, leadership skill is a must for every professional. Leadership skill is not meant just only for leaders or managers. Anybody can be a good leader. It's not just about monitoring or managing others when you have good leadership qualities. Instead, communicate to your coworkers and managers about your plan and vision, support them, and embrace their ideas and suggestions. It's extremely crucial to be self-aware and hold yourself accountable. To become a better leader, it is important to improve writing and communication skills, as well as knowledge and comprehension of public relations, advertising, research, negotiation, and management. In addition, flexibility and adaptability are essential skills that are required by supply chain professionals. Businesses throughout the world are seeing flexibility and adaptability as significant skills, particularly during COVID-19. Even after post-COVID-19, this new way of conducting business is likely to persist. Being flexible at work used to imply a lot of traveling around. It's now more about keeping an open mind, working well under pressure, adapting to new and unexpected deadlines, prioritizing tasks, and taking on additional responsibilities.

Critical thinking ability is the third must-have skill. According to the Society for Human Resource Management (SHRM), more than three-quarters of employers claimed they didn't hire people because they didn't have adequate problem-solving and critical thinking abilities. In today's world, it's critical to be able to think clearly and rationally while objectively evaluating information in order to make informed decisions. Good critical thinkers elicit more information from the information they're reading by asking questions. Hence, critical thinking and cultural awareness are critical skills to have when working within international relations. No doubt, technology savvy is a necessary skill in today's business world. Even before the COVID-19, it was evident that there was a global shortage of digital skills in the business environment. The majority of jobs today need some level of digital proficiency. The COVID-19 has made it even more critical for firms to hire digital professionals with unique skills to assist them in adapting to all of today's emerging technology and platforms. It's critical to invest in people who understand how to use technology in the Fourth Industrial Revolution (4IR). Big data, blockchain, data literacy, computer programming, AI and a variety of other technical skills will be advantageous.

Furthermore, communication and emotional intelligence are two skills that supply chain professionals should possess. This implies that communication and emotional intelligence are inextricably linked. There is still a need for genuine personal connection and understanding in every job. Thus, awareness and empathy for other people's feelings and behaviors are important, particularly in creating customer loyalty. It's also crucial to have solid communication skills in this situation. As more individuals work from home, it's more important than ever to be explicit in emails and virtual meetings to maintain trust and productivity.

Last but not least, supply chain professionals have also required creativity and innovation skills. Although there have been many advancements in analytics and commercial operations, the one who is capable of thinking beyond the box will remain relevant in the industry. Creativity is critical in all industries and fields. In the coming years, it will be critical for firms to alter and adapt fast. Anyone who wants to work in business, for example, will need to be able to think outside the box in order to assist their firm to solve problems and taking advantage of possibilities.

Is there anything that you would like to add to be a competent supply chain manager?

Without any prior experience, Bangladesh's freight and logistics business arose in 1991 to 1992 and struggled due to a lack of competent labor and essential communication skills. Despite the lack of proper government regulations and policies, as well as inexperienced exporters and importers, the industry has grown in importance. According to Bangladesh Bank data, imported goods worth US$52.84 billion and exported products worth US$36.67 billion during the fiscal year 2017 to 2018. During the last 30 years, the country has also directly generated over 40,000 employments, making it one of the most important industries contributing to the country's economic growth. Bangladesh was named one of the 45 main emerging markets in the globe by Kuwait-based Agility Global Integrated Logistics "The Agility Emerging Markets Logistics Index (AEMLI)" 2018. The country's logistics industry was rated as highly progressive by the Index, but it noted that the country faces major challenges, including the need for infrastructure improvements, diversification away from the apparel sector, and improvements in the pharmaceutical, steel, shipbuilding, and food processing industries in order to achieve exponential market share in the future. To fulfill the needs of its developing economy and enhance export growth, the country must also improve ways to strengthen its transportation and logistics infrastructure. In addition, skilled practitioners are also a necessity to bring the industry to the next level. Thus, reskilling and upskilling are the important strategy to remain competitive. Bangladesh may considerably increase export growth by stressing the logistics business more effectively.

Interview from Pakistan

SereneAir (Pvt.) Ltd.

Company Overview

SereneAir was established in the commercial aviation sector of Pakistan in 2016 and started its flight operations from January 2017. The purpose was to fill the void that existed in the domestic air transport market as well as to tap the opportunity in the international market segments. SereneAir was established as the third private airline in Pakistan in addition to PIA the National Flag carrier. Since the beginning SereneAir captured around 30% of domestic revenue due to its smart operation and maintenance planning. It achieved 99% serviceability rate and over 98% dispatch rate. This was a key success factor. Success was achieved with the operation of only three narrow body aircraft. However, within next 2 years, one of the competitor, that is, Shaheen Air quit the market and pave the way for expansion to other players. SereneAir capitalized that opportunity and decided to add two more aircraft in its fleet in 2019. However, 2020 to 2021 posed quite a bit of drag to its progress due to COVID-19 and its negative effects on worldwide aviation industry. Despite the challenges, SereneAir successfully flew four narrow body and three wide body aircraft on domestics and international destinations. Mr Syed Yousuf is head of SCM and the manager for southern region.

Key Goals for SCM Department

Supply Chain Department of SereneAir was initially named as P&L and has been tasked to work out the initial requirement of the Airline with close coordination of other two departments, that is, Maintenance and Operation. The prime task was to operate the airline with lean and smart logistics support with minimum possible investment in the inventory and support equipment. The task has been successfully accomplished by adopting Just-in-Time (JIT) concept of material support. To cater for other technical and operational services, third party memorandums of understanding were signed with support entities already present at the aerodrome. Technical equipment support was made with PIA, Ground Support Services with Royal Airport Services and a few more agreements were signed both domestically and overseas. The SCM department was made responsible for the following areas:

(a) Initial planning for procurement of essentially needed equipment/tools/component/spares parts and related expendables/consumables for maintenance support activities.
(b) Sourcing of aviation items, short listings, and getting technical approval as per ICAO standards and best practices before order placement.
(c) Close liaison with Finance Department and banks for timely payment to all vendors across the globe.
(d) Transport arrangement of procured items from all across the world through freight forwarders/couriers.
(e) Custom clearance and timely availability of needed components right at the time of its requirement to ensure optimum serviceability of all aircraft fleet.
(f) All the personnel (over 450) had to be equipped with uniform/clothing as per approved design and specified standards.

(g) Coordination with Tech and Ops for design and approval of forms/tags/display charts/boarding passes/stationery and other essential office equipment/tools, and so on.
(h) Sourcing/purchase and provision of cabin facilitation items as per aviation standards and best practices.
(i) Sourcing and supplies of catering/food items through third party agreement.

The above were the initial tasks that were assigned and achieved by SCM department. Continuity of support, and sustainability of maintenance, and successful operation of flights are the major goals entrusted with SCM department.

Skills and Competencies to Meet the Department Goals

Establishing a Support Department for an airline from scratch is a gigantic task and it needs well-qualified and experienced staff in the related fields. This challenge was entrusted by the CEO to the head of SCM department having core competencies in the aviation support management (SCM) with adequate experience in the aviation sector. The head selected a team having airline experience in the segment of warehousing and inventory management at the execution level and hired fresh graduate engineers for the technical procurement. After a short in-house training, the staff went into operation under a very close supervision. However, on-the-job training (OJT) continued as per the CAA requirement, and gradually skills and competencies of the new hires were developed to the desired level. The enhancement of professional qualification has been encouraged and three of procurement staff earned International Supply Chain Certification as certified professionals. Another one is undergoing a Master program in SCM from Institute of Business Administration (IBM) Karachi. In addition to above about half a dozen personnel are hired and trained in-house for purchase and support management of general items for cabin supplies and catering support supervision. The Supply Chain Department of SereneAir started functioning with only two experienced personnel and within 5 years it is functioning with six well-trained managers having international qualification in the field of SCM.

Future Skills and Competencies to Meet Future Needs

Functional competency of supply chain in the aviation industry is somewhat different from other industries. The competency requirement directly depends on various factors like, regulatory restrictions on movement of sensitive components from one region to another, import policies by the respective governments, State Bank's restrictions on transfer of money, Custom policies and conditions on clearance of stores, and so on. These policies and regulations keep changing from time to time. SCM professionals must be cognizant of all applicable limitations along with international political landscape and economic scenarios. Therefore, no specific competency or skill can be foreseen to prepare any lot available to meet the future requirement, unless otherwise work force be deployed to get OJT in real-time conditions and changing scenarios. However, fundamental knowledge on different functions of SCM would be helpful in quick understanding of the job requirements to fulfill operational commitments as assigned by higher management.

Was there any specific skill needed to work during the pandemic period?

In the aviation industry everything moves physically; therefore, all precautions as deemed necessary to work during pandemic were adopted. Hardly anything like work from home is applicable in this industry. During the recent pandemic period, the employees of SereneAir kept working while following necessary precautions and ensuring timely availability of aircraft as per operational demand. Traveling of passengers was restricted and required tests and permission by the concerned authorities. The airlines operated passenger aircraft for transportation of goods during the pandemic period. SereneAir inducted two wide-body aircraft during the pandemic period as cargo business was increasing leaps and bounds.

References

Agami, N., Mohamed, S., and Mohamed, R. (2012). Supply chain performance measurement approaches: Review and classification. *Journal of Organizational Management Studies*, 1–20. DOI: 10.5171/2012.872753.

Ahmed, E. B., Nabli, A., and Gargouri, F. (2013). Group extraction from professional social network using a new semi-supervised hierarchical clustering. *Knowledge and Information Systems,* 40(1), 29–47. DOI: 10.1007/s10115-013-0634-x.

Al-Futtaim (2022). About Al-Futtaim Logistics. https://www.aflogistics.com/about-us/.

Al Ahbabi, S. A., Singh, S. K., Balasubramanian, S., and Gaur, S. S. (2019). Employee perception of the impact of knowledge management processes on public sector performance. *Journal of Knowledge Management*, 23(2), 351–373. DOI: 10.1108/JKM-08-2017-0348.

Alruwaili, F., and Alahmadi, D. (2021). Enhanced clustering-based MOOC recommendations using LinkedIn Profiles (MR-LI). *International Journal of Advanced Computer Science and Applications,* 12(8), 151–160. DOI: 10.14569/ijacsa.2021.0120818.

Anderson, J. C., and Gerbing, D. W. (1988). Structural equation modeling in practice: A review and recommended two-step approach. *Psychological Bulletin,* 103(3), 411–423. DOI: 10.1037/0033-2909.103.3.411.

APICS. (2009). Supply chain manager competency model. http://www.apics.org/docs/default-source/careers-competency-models/supply-chain-manager-competency-model.pdf.

Athey, T. R., and Orth, M. S. (1999). Emerging competency methods for the future." *Human Resource Management,* 38(3), 215–225. DOI: 10.1002/(sici)1099-050x(199923)38:33.0.co;2-w.

Balasubramanian, S., and Shukla, V. (2017). Green supply chain management: An empirical investigation on the construction sector. *Supply*

Chain Management: An International Journal, 22(1), 58–81. DOI: 10.1108/SCM-07-2016-0227.

Barnes, J., and Liao, Y. (2012). The effect of individual, network, and collaborative competencies on the supply chain management system. *International Journal of Production Economics,* 140(2), 888–899. DOI: 10.1016/j.ijpe.2012.07.010.

BCG. (2021). Changer in the fight against climate change. https://www.bcg.com/publications/2021/fighting-climate-change-with-supply-chain-decarbonization.

Boudreau, J. W. (2003). On the Interface Between Operations and Human Resources Management. *Manufacturing & Service Operations Management,* 5(3), 179–267. DOI: 10.1287/msom.5.3.179.16032.

Caplice, C. (2005). Time to take the lead. *Traffic World,* 269(33), 19–21.

Carter, C. R., Leuschner, R., and Rogers, D. S. (2007). A social network analysis of the *Journal of Supply Chain Management*: Knowledge generation, knowledge diffusion and thought leadership. *Journal of Supply Chain Management,* 43(2), 15–28. DOI: 10.1111/j.1745-493x.2007.00028.x.

Case, T., Gardiner, A., Rutner, P., and Dyer, J. (2013). A LinkedIn analysis of career paths of information systems alumni. *Journal of the Southern Association Information Systems,* 1(1). DOI: 10.3998/jsais.11880084.0001.102.

Chen, I. J., and Paulraj, A. (2004). Understanding supply chain management: critical research and a theoretical framework. *International Journal of Production Research,* 42(1), 131–163. DOI: 10.1080/0020754031000l602865.

Christopher, M. (1999). Logistics and supply chain management: Strategies for reducing cost and improving service (Second Edition). *International Journal of Logistics Research and Applications,* 2(1), 103–104. DOI: 10.1080/13675569908901575.

CIPS. (2019). The role of soft skills in SCM. https://www.cips.org/supply-management/opinion/2019/may/the-role-of-soft-skills-in-scm/.

Closs, D. J. (2000). Preface. *Journal of Business Logistics,* 21(1), i–iii.

Closs, D. J., and Mollenkopf, D. A. (2004). A global supply chain framework. *Industrial Marketing Management,* 33(1), 37–44. DOI: 10.1016/j.indmarman.2003.08.008.

Dai, K., Nespereira, C., Vilas, A. and Díaz Redondo, R. (2015). Scraping and Clustering Techniques for the Characterization of Linkedin Profiles. DOI: 10.5121/csit.2015.50101.

Davis, J., Wolff, H.-G., Forret, M. L., and Sullivan, S. E. (2020). Networking via LinkedIn: An examination of usage and career benefits. *Journal of Vocational Behavior*, 118, 103396. DOI: 10.1016/j.jvb.2020.103396.

de Gottal, A., and Bonny, G. (2019). In the long run, will LinkedIn's services endanger or assist recruitment and placement agencies in Belgium? Could there be a win-win situation? Louvain School of Management, Université catholique de Louvain. http://hdl.handle.net/2078.1/thesis:21057.

DHL. (2021). The Deepening Talent Shortage. https://www.dhl.com/content/dam/dhl/global/dhl-supply-chain/documents/pdf/dhl--glo-sci-x-sector-talent-shortage.pdf.

Dubai Chamber of Commerce (2021). Online F&B Sales in UAE surge 255% in 2020: Analysis. https://www.dubaichamber.com/whats-happening/chamber_news/online-fb-sales-in-uae-surge-255-in-2020-analysis.

Dubey, R., and Gunasekaran, A. (2015). Supply chain talent: The missing link in supply chain strategy. *Industrial and Commercial Training*, 47(5), 257–264. DOI: 10.1108/ICT-11-2014-0073.

Ellinger, A. E., and Ellinger, A. D. (2014). Leveraging human resource development expertise to improve supply chain managers' skills and competencies. *European Journal of Training and Development*, 38(1/2), 118–135. DOI: 10.1108/EJTD-09-2013-0093.

Ernst & Young (EY) US. How disruption has reframed the future of work in supply chains. EY US-Building a Better Working World. Last modified April 8, 2021. https://www.ey.com.

Forbes. (2018). Supply chain talent shortage: What's an industry to do? https://www.forbes.com/sites/oracle/2018/04/17/supply-chain-talent-shortage-whats-an-industry-to-do/?sh=55d10bdc791d.

Forbes. (2021). The circular supply chain: A push for sustainability. https://www.forbes.com/sites/stevebanker/2021/06/29/the-circular-supply-chain-a-push-for-sustainability/?sh=6779685537c1.

Gammelgaard, B., and Larson, P. D. (2001). Logistics skills and competencies for supply chain management. *Journal of Business logistics*, 22(2), 27–50. DOI: 10.1002/j.2158-1592.2001.tb00002.x.

Gibson, B., Gibson, M., and Rutner, S. (1998). *Careers in Logistics.* Council of Supply Chain Management Professionals.

Green, K. W., Inman, R. A., Sower, V. E., and Zelbst, P. J. (2019). Comprehensive supply chain management model. *Supply Chain Management: An International Journal*, 24(5), 590–603. DOI: 10.1108/scm-12-2018-0441.

Hammer, M. (1990). Reengineering Work: Don't Automate, Obliterate. *Harvard Business Review*, July–August, 104–112.

Herden, T. T. (2020). Explaining the competitive advantage generated from analytics with the knowledge-based view: The example of logistics and supply chain management. *Business Research*, 13, 163–214. DOI: 10.1007/s40685-019-00104-x.

Hofmann, E., and Rüsch, M. (2017). Industry 4.0 and the current status as well as future prospects on logistics. *Computers in Industry*, 89, 23–34. DOI: 10.1016/j.compind.2017.04.002.

Hoffman, W. (2005). Logistics' evolving curriculum. *Traffic World*, 269, no. 2, 19–21.

Hofmann, E., Sternberg, H., Chen, H., Pflaum, A., and Prockl, G. (2019). Supply chain management and Industry 4.0: Conducting research in the digital age. *International Journal of Physical Distribution & Logistics Management*, 49(10), 945–955. DOI: 10.1108/IJPDLM-11-2019-399.

Hotel & Catering News Middle East (2021). The Big Chill, Cold Chain Fulfilment. https://www.hotelnewsme.com/hotel-news-me/the-big-chill-cold-chain-fulfilment/.

Ibrahim, R., Boerhannoeddin, A., and Bakare, K. K. (2017). The effect of soft skills and training methodology on employee performance. *European Journal of Training and Development*, 41(4), 388–406. DOI: 10.1108/EJTD-08-2016-0066.

ICC UAE (2022). Al Futtaim Logistics Company LLC — ICC UAE. https://iccuae.com/0108.html.

John, G. (2015). *Developing Supply Chain Capability — Findings of the Talent Survey 2015*. London: SCMWorld.

Kauffeld, S. (2006). Self-directed work groups and team competence. *Journal of Occupational and Organizational Psychology*, 79(1), 1–21. DOI: 10.1348/096317905x53237.

Khan, S. A. R., Zhang, Y., Kumar, A., Zavadskas, E., and Streimikiene, D. (2020). Measuring the impact of renewable energy, public health expenditure, logistics, and environmental performance on sustainable economic growth. *Sustainable Development* , 28(4), 833–843. DOI: 10.1002/sd.2034.

Koufteros, X. A., Rawski, G. E., and Rupak, R. (2010). Organizational integration for product development: the effects on glitches, on-time execution of engineering change orders, and market success. *Decision Sciences*, 41(1), 49–80. DOI: 10.1111/j.1540- 5915.2009.00259.x.

La Londe, B. J. (1990). Update logistics skills for the future. *Transportation and Distribution*, 16–48.

Lai, K.-H., Ngai, E. W. T., and Cheng, T. C. E. (2002). Measures for evaluating supply chain performance in transport logistics. *Transportation Research Part E: Logistics and Transportation Review*, 38(6), 439–456. DOI: 10.1016/s1366-5545(02)00019-4.

Lawler, E. E. (1994). From job-based to competency-based organizations. *Journal of Organizational Behavior*, 15(1), 3–15. DOI: 10.1002/job.4030150103.

LeMay, S. A. (1999). *The Growth and Development of Logistics Personnel.* Council of Supply Chain Management Professionals.

Li, S., Ragu-Nathan, B., Ragu-Nathan, T. S., and Subba Rao, S. (2006). The impact of supply chain management practices on competitive advantage and organizational performance. *Omega*, 34(2), 107–124. DOI: 10.1016/j.omega.2004.08.002.

Logistics & Transport Middle East (2021). Al-Futtaim Logistics Deploys Smart Technology for Greater Productivity. https://www.transportandlogisticsme.com/smart-logistics/al-futtaim-logistics-deploys-smart-technology-for-greater-efficiency.

Logistics ME (2021). In conversation with Dr. Raman Kumar, Managing Director at Al-Futtaim Logistics. https://www.youtube.com/watch?v=-JQ0XC9AQMMQ.

Luthra, S., Govindan, K., Kannan, D., Mangla, S. K., and Garg, C. P. (2017). An integrated framework for sustainable supplier selection and evaluation in supply chains. *Journal of Cleaner Production*, 140(3), 1686–1698. DOI: 10.1016/j.jclepro.2016.09.078.

Mangan, J., and Christopher, M. (2005). Management development and the supply chain manager of the future. *The International Journal of Logistics Management*, 16(2), 178–191. DOI: 10.1108/09574090510634494.

McCarter, M. W., and Northcraft, G. B. (2007). Happy together? *Journal of Operations Management*, 25(2), 498–511. DOI: 10.1016/j.jom.2006.05.005.

McClelland, D. C. (1973). Testing for competence rather than for "intelligence." *American Psychologist*, 28(1), 1–14. DOI: 10.1037/h0034092.

McKinsey. Next generation supply chain: Supply chain (2020). McKinsey & Company | Global Management Consulting. Last modified 2013. https://www.mckinsey.com.

Mid-east information (2021). Al-Futtaim Logistics Wins Cold Chain Service Provider of the Year Award. https://mid-east.info/al-futtaim-logistics-wins-cold-chain-service-provider-of-the-year-award/.

MIDA. (2021). Malaysia listed among top ten in global logistics ranking. https://www.mida.gov.my/mida-news/malaysia-listed-among-top-ten-in-global-logistics-ranking/.

Minahan, T. (1998). How the supply chain changes your job. *Purchasing*, 124(2), 57–58.

Mirabile, R. (1997). Everything you wanted to know about competency modeling. *Training and Development*, 51(8), 73–77.

Mordor Intelligence. (2022). Malaysia freight and logistics market — Growth, trends, COVID-19 impact, and forecasts (2021–2027). https://www.mordorintelligence.com/industry-reports/malaysia-freight-logistics-market-study.

Murphy, P. R., and Poist, R. F. (1991a). A comparison of headhunter and practitioner views regarding skill requirements of senior-level logistics professionals. *Logistics and Transportation Review*, 27(3), 277–294.

Murphy, P. R., and Poist, R. F. (1991b). Skill requirements of senior-level logisticians: Practitioner perspectives. *International Journal of Physical Distribution & Logistics Management*, 21(3), 3–14. DOI: 10.1108/09600039110004025.

Murphy, P. R., and Poist, R. F. (2006). Skill requirements of contemporary senior- and entry-level logistics managers: A comparative analysis. *Transportation Journal*, 45(3), 46–60.

Murphy, P. R., and Poist, R. F. (2007). Skill requirements of senior-level logisticians: A longitudinal assessment. *Supply Chain Management: An International Journal*, 12(6), 423–431. DOI: 10.1108/13598540710826353.

Myers, M. B., Griffith, D. A., Daugherty, P. J., and Lusch, R. F. (2004). Maximizing the human capital equation in logistics: Education, experience, and skills. *Journal of Business Logistics*, 25(1), 211–232. DOI: 10.1002/j.2158-1592.2004.tb00175.x.

National Fourth Industrial Revolution Policy. (2021). https://www.mida.gov.my.

Nayal, P., Pandey, N., and Paul, J. (2021). Covid-19 pandemic and consumer-employee-organization wellbeing: A dynamic capability theory approach. *Journal of Consumer Affairs*, 56(1), 359–390. DOI: 10.1111/joca.12399.

Oracle. (2021). Industry 4.0 and SCM. https://www.oracle.com/ae/scm/what-is-supply-chain-management/.

Parry, S. (1996). The quest for competence. *Training*, 33(7), 48–54.

Pekovic, S., and Rolland, S. (2020). Recipes for achieving customer loyalty: A qualitative comparative analysis of the dimensions of customer experience. *Journal of Retailing and Consumer Services*, 56, 102171. DOI: 10.1016/j.jretconser.2020.102.

Pham, T. (2021). Reconceptualizing employability of returnees: What really matters and strategic navigating approaches. *Higher Education,* 81, 1329–1345. DOI: 10.1007/s10734-020-00614-2.

Poist, R. F. (1984). Managing logistics in an era of change. *Defence Transportation Journal*, 23–30.

Prajogo, D., and Sohal, A. (2013). Supply chain professionals: A study of competencies, use of technologies, and future challenges. *International Journal of Operations & Production Management*, 33(11/12), 1532–1554. DOI: 10.1108/IJOPM-08-2010-0228.

Prieto, V. M., Manuel, A., and Cacheda, F. (2013). Detecting Linkedin spammers and its spam nets. *International Journal of Advanced Computer Science and Applications*, 4(9), 189–199. DOI: 10.14569/ijacsa.2013.040930.

Razzaque, A. M., and Sirat, M. S. B. (2001). Skill requirements: Perception of the senior Asian logisticians. *International Journal of Physical Distribution & Logistics Management,* 31(5), 374–395. DOI: 10.1108/09600030110395175.

Rodrigues, D., and Martinez, L. F. (2020). The influence of digital marketing on recruitment effectiveness: a qualitative study. *European Journal of Management Studies*, 25(1), 23–44. DOI: 10.1108/EJMS-09-2020-002.

Sawyerr, E., and Harrison, C. (2020). Developing resilient supply chains: Lessons from high-reliability organisations. *Supply Chain Management*, 25(1), 77–100. DOI: 10.1108/SCM-09-2018-0329.

Shou, Y., and Wang, W. (2017). Multidimensional competences of supply chain managers: An empirical study. *Enterprise Information Systems*, 11(1), 58–74. DOI: 10.1080/17517575.2015.1080303.

Simatupang, T. M., and Sridharan, R. (2002). The collaborative supply chain. *The International Journal of Logistics Management,* 13(1), 15–30. DOI: 10.1108/09574090210806333.

Siwar, C., Ahmed, F., Bashawir, A., and Mia, M. S. (2016). Urbanization and urban poverty in Malaysia: Consequences and vulnerability. *Journal of Applied Sciences*, 16(4), 154–160. DOI: 10.3923/jas.2016.154.160.

Sutduean, J., Harakan, A., and Jermsittiparsert, K. (2019). Exploring the nexus between supply chain integration, export marketing strategies practices and export performance: A case of Indonesian firms. *Humanities & Social Sciences Reviews,* 7(3), 711–719. DOI: 10.18510/hssr.2019.73102.

Tan, L. M., and Laswad, F. (2018). Professional skills required of accountants: What do job advertisements tell us? *Accounting Education*, 27(4), 403–432.

Tatham, P., Wu, Y., Kovács, G., and Butcher, T. (2017). Supply chain management skills to sense and seize opportunities. *The International Journal of Logistics Management*, 28(2), 266–289. DOI: 10.1108/IJLM-04-2014-0066.

Thai, V. V., Ibrahim, K. B., Vidya, R., and Huang, H. Y. (2012). Competency profile of managers in the Singapore logistics industry. *The Asian Journal of Shipping and Logistics*, 28(2), 161–182. DOI: 10.1016/j.ajsl.2012.08.002.

Thai, Vinh V., Cahoon, S., and Tran, H. T. (2011). Skill requirements for logistics professionals: Findings and implications. *Asia Pacific Journal of Marketing and Logistics*, 23(4), 553–574. DOI: 10.1108/13555851111165084.

The CEO Magazine (2020). Remarkably fast: Raman Kumar. https://www.theceomagazine.com/executive-interviews/transportation-logistics/raman-kumar/.

Trunick, P. A. (1998). New demands for tomorrow's manager. *Transportation and Distribution*, 18–19.

Twelfth Malaysia Plan, 2021-2025. (2021). https://rmke12.epu.gov.my/bm.

Wahab, S. N., Rajendran, S. D., and Yeap, S. P. (2021). Upskilling and reskilling requirement in logistics and supply chain industry for the fourth industrial revolution. *LogForum*, 17(3), 399–410.

Williams, A. W., and Currey, P. (1990). Desired attributes of logistics managers and a learning hierarchy in management education. *Logistics and Transportation Review*, 26(4), 369–379.

Wu, Y.-C., Lee, H.-M., and Liao, P.-R. (2018). What do customers expect of travel agent–customer interactions? Measuring and improving customer experience in interactions with travel agents. *Journal of Travel & Tourism Marketing*, 35(8), 1–13. DOI: 10.1080/10548408.2018.1468853.

Young, L. (1998). Human element. *Materials Management and Distribution*, 27.

www.ingramcontent.com/pod-product-compliance
Lightning Source LLC
Chambersburg PA
CBHW050628190326
41458CB00008B/2188

* 9 7 8 9 8 1 1 2 5 8 8 4 8 *